THE COMMON L~ D1435158

McGREGOR

ON

DAMAGES

Second Supplement
to the
Nineteenth Edition

Up-to-date to August 2016

BY

JAMES EDELMAN

Justice of the Federal Court of Australia

AND

HARVEY McGREGOR

CBE, Q.C., D.C.L., S.J.D.

CHAPTER ON THE HUMAN RIGHTS ACT
CONTRIBUTED BY MARTIN SPENCER Q.C.

CHAPTERS ON PROCEDURE
REVISED BY JULIAN PICTON Q.C.

SWEET & MAXWELL

THOMSON REUTERS

Published in 2016 by Thomson Reuters (Professional) UK Limited
trading as Sweet & Maxwell,
Friars House, 160 Blackfriars Road, London, SE1 8EZ
(Registered in England & Wales, Company No 1679046.
Registered Office and address for service:
2nd floor, 1 Mark Square, Leonard Street, London EC2A 4EG)

For further information on our products and services, visit:
http://www.sweetandmaxwell.co.uk
Typeset by Wright and Round Ltd., Gloucestershire
Printed and bound in Great Britain by CPI Group (UK) Ltd, Croydon, CR0 4YY

No natural forests were destroyed to make this product;
only farmed timber was used and re-planted.

British Library Cataloguing in Publication Data

A CIP catalogue record for this book
is available from the British Library

ISBN 978-0-41406-100-2

HOW TO USE THIS SUPPLEMENT

This is the Second Supplement to the Nineteenth Edition of
McGregor on Damages, and has been compiled according to the
structure of the main volume.

At the beginning of each chapter of this Supplement is an abbreviated table
of contents from the main volume. Where a heading in this table of
contents has been marked by the symbol ■, this indicates that there is
relevant information in the Supplement to which the reader should refer.
Material that has been included from the previous Supplement is indicated
by the symbol □.

Within each chapter, updating information is referenced to
the relevant paragraph in the main volume.

ACKNOWLEDGEMENT

In 1961, Harvey McGregor produced the 12th edition of what was then known as *Mayne and McGregor on Damages*. Many developments had occurred in the law of damages during the quarter century since the previous edition. Consequently, there was a great deal more of McGregor's work in the 12th edition than there was from Mayne. Harvey was so much more than just an exceptional lawyer. But he became known worldwide for his fine legal acumen. Over the next 54 years *McGregor on Damages* became the work for which Harvey rightly received acclaim as the world's leading authority on damages.

In late October 2014, Harvey contacted me to ask if I would consider taking over *McGregor on Damages* after the 20th edition. I had rejected the same enquiry, years earlier, when it was made through a mutual acquaintance. But times had changed and my academic commitments had nearly vanished. Harvey wanted the book to be written by a single author. He said, and I agree, that "the great merit of the book is that its vast substance is written by a single person so that all the parts dovetail". Harvey was also in excellent health. Both he and I thought that this would mean a handover some time in 2019. That was not to be. Unfortunately, on 27 June 2015, Harvey passed away. Characteristically, he had been working on this supplement until very shortly before his death.

Although my association with Harvey was very brief, it has been an honour to be able to complete this supplement and to continue Harvey's *magnum opus*. One story suffices here to describe Harvey's deep learning, his characteristic generosity, and his kindness. In July 2000, I had just completed a draft of my doctorate on gain-based damages. In that month, the House of Lords delivered its decision in *Attorney General v Blake* [2001] 1 A.C. 268. That decision lead to much revision and rewriting. I had been immersed in the decision for several months when Harvey came to Oxford to speak on damages issues, including on the *Blake* decision. The room at New College was packed to the rafters. Harvey was very critical of *Blake*. In my thesis, however, I lauded it. At the conclusion of his presentation I asked a series of questions designed to defend the decision. Harvey responded softly and politely explaining that damages and compensation were synonyms. The latter was not a species of the former. His answer was steeped in the learning of half a century's work on damages. None of his answer changed anything in my doctorate. My work was much the poorer for not understanding the nuances in his answer. Harvey's speech, his answers to my questions 15 years ago, and his subsequent writing, were strong factors in my understanding of the error in my thinking that a party who deliberately breaches a contract should, without more, often have to disgorge profits. The context of *Blake* was fundamentally important, in particular Lord Nicholls' much neglected comment that George Blake's undertaking was either a fiduciary obligation or was closely akin to one. Much may therefore depend upon the relationship between contractual and fiduciary obligations. As a great scholar, Harvey's work was also constantly moving. His doubts about the *Blake* decision became more muted. By the 19th edition of *McGregor on Damages* the scare quotes had been removed from the phrase restitutionary damages. Chapter 14 now contains, in part, a defence of gain-based damages, although one which plays close attention to the factual circumstances of various categories of case. And, on the issue of whether it matters to have a characterisation of obligations as either contractual (common law) or fiduciary (equity), the 19th edition now begins with the sentence: "Damages are now defined in this book quite simply as an award in money for a civil wrong."

I will write more about Harvey in the preface to the 20th edition of *McGregor on Damages*, which will also commence with an acknowledgement from one of his learned colleagues. Nevertheless, it was necessary for me to begin this second supplement with these introductory words to acknowledge the debt that I, like all others in the legal profession, owe to Harvey. My debt will only be repaid in part by an attempt to maintain the quality and integrity of the work, which should always remain as *McGregor on Damages*.

JAMES EDELMAN
August 2016

CONTENTS

BOOK ONE
COMPENSATORY DAMAGES

BOOK TWO
NON-COMPENSATORY DAMAGES

BOOK THREE
VARIOUS GENERAL FACTORS IN THE
ASSESSMENT OF DAMAGES

BOOK FOUR
PARTICULAR CONTRACTS AND TORTS

BOOK SIX
PROCEDURE

TABLE OF CASES

TABLE OF STATUTES

TABLE OF STATUTORY INSTRUMENTS

TABLE OF CIVIL PROCEDURE RULES

INTRODUCTORY

1. A DEFINITION OF DAMAGES

(3) *The omission of the reference to tort and breach of contract*

Change the heading to read: **(a) Damages under the Human Rights Act and other statutes**   **1–012**

Insert a new paragraph after para.1–012:

Apart from the major area of claims concerning damages for breaches of the **1–012A** Human Rights Act, there are many other statutes which confer rights to damages. This book does not deal with all of those statutes. This is because the principles to be applied in each case can be heavily dependent upon statutory text, context and purpose rather than upon underlying common law norms. For instance, in *The Mayor's Office for Policing and Crime v Mitsui Sumitomo Insurance Co (Europe) Ltd & Ors* [2016] UKSC 18, the Supreme Court considered the meaning of the words "sustained loss by such injury, stealing, or destruction" in s.2 of the Riot (Damages) Act 1886. The court held that the word "loss" did not include consequential losses. Instead, at [34], the court said that the statute was "a self-contained statutory scheme which did not mirror the common law of tort".

Insert a new paragraph after para.1–016:

It must, however, be acknowledged that this position is becoming increasingly **1–016A** difficult to maintain. The observations of Lord Browne-Wilkinson in *Target Holdings v Redferns*, quoted in the paragraph above, if applied as an absolute proposition would not be consistent with those of Lord Toulson in *AIB Group (UK) Plc v Mark Redler & Co Solicitors* [2014] UKSC 58; [2014] 3 W.L.R. 1367 at [59], who observed that in *Bank of New Zealand v New Zealand Guardian*

Trust Co Ltd [1999] 1 NZLR 664 Tipping J had "rightly observed that while historically the law has tended to place emphasis on the legal characterisation of the relationship between the parties in delineating the remedies available for breach of an obligation, the nature of the duty which has been breached can often be more important, when considering issues of causation and remoteness, than the classification or historical source of the obligation". More recently, in *Daniel v Tee* [2016] EWHC 1538 (Ch), Richard Spearman QC sitting as a Deputy High Court judge, although finding no liability for breach of trust in that case, said that "although equitable compensation and common law damages are remedies based on separate legal obligations, the broad aim of both remedies is the same" ([53]) and "where claims for negligence, breach of contract and breach of trust arise out of the same facts, the level of compensation recoverable under each head of claim may be held to be the same" ([55]). Then at [55], quoting from *AIB Group (UK) plc v Mark Redler & Co Solicitors* [2014] UKSC 58, Lord Reed SCJ at [136]-[137]:

> "Those structural similarities do not however entail that the relevant rules are identical: as in mathematics, isomorphism is not the same as equality. As courts around the world have accepted, a trust imposes different obligations from a contractual or tortious relationship, in the setting of a different kind of relationship. The law responds to those differences by allowing a measure of compensation for breach of trust causing loss to the trust fund which reflects the nature of the obligation breached and the relationship between the parties . . . "

BOOK ONE

COMPENSATORY DAMAGES

BOOK ONE

PART ONE

OBJECT AND TERMINOLOGY

THE OBJECT OF AN AWARD OF COMPENSATORY DAMAGES

(3) *Compensation greater than loss*

Insert a new paragraph and heading after para.2–007:

(4) *Compensation is not discretionary*

It follows from the previous discussion that an award of compensatory dam- **2–008**
ages is made as a matter of right. It is not a matter of discretion. Even when a
right to compensatory damages is created by statute, the use of permissive words
like "may award damages" is unlikely to be understood as creating the radical
change of making compensatory damages a matter of judicial discretion. This
issue was decided as a preliminary issue in *Energy Solutions EU Ltd v Nuclear
Decommissioning Authority* [2015] EWCA 1262. In that case, the primary judge
was concerned with a claim for damages under reg.47J(2)(c) of the Public
Contracts Regulations 2006 which provides that a court "*may* award damages to
an economic operator which has suffered loss or damage as a consequence of the
breach". Edwards-Stuart J held, at [93], that much clearer wording than the mere
use of "may" was needed before the Regulations would be held to introduce the
novel concept of discretionary damages.

CHAPTER 3

TERMINOLOGY USED IN COMPENSATORY DAMAGES AWARDS

(2) *Normal and consequential losses*

Remove the last sentence beginning with "With our doctrine of precedent . . . " **3–016**
and replace it with the following: The pathway to a new approach has been paved
in *Transocean Drilling (UK) Ltd v Providence Resources Plc* [2016] EWCA Civ
372, Transocean contracted with Providence for Transocean to provide its semi-
submersible drilling rig for use by Providence. Transocean breached its contract
by failing to supply the rig in good working condition. Providence suffered losses
from additional overheads as a result of the delay (wasted costs of personnel,
equipment, and third party services). The short issue on the appeal was whether
these overhead costs were "consequential losses" which had been excluded by
clause 20 of the contract. There were two limbs of clause 20. The first was
concerned with "any indirect or consequential loss or damages under English
law". The critical words of the second limb of clause 20 applied to exclude the
following to the extent that the first limb did not apply: " . . . loss of use
(including, without limitation, loss of use or the cost of use of property, equipment, materials and services including without limitation, those provided by
contractors or subcontractors of every tier or by third parties), loss of business
and business interruption". It was conceded that the first limb did not apply. The
Court of Appeal held that the loss fell within the meaning of the second limb.
Moore-Bick LJ delivered the decision with which the other Lord Justices agreed.
He explained the difficulties that the expression "consequential loss" had caused
in English law and questioned whether the modern English decisions described
above would be decided in the same way today once it is accepted that the
meaning of expressions like "consequential loss" depends upon particular context. So much can be immediately accepted. However, the particular context of
clause 20 was unusually rich with detail. This is not common. A mere reference
to "consequential loss" should still permit the starting point of the courts to be
that the losses which have been excluded are all those losses which are not the
"normal loss" that would be suffered by any claimant in that position.

BOOK ONE

PART TWO

THE HEADS OF COMPENSATORY DAMAGES

CHAPTER 5

NON-PECUNIARY LOSSES

I. TORT

NOTE 4: Add at the end of the note: Since these procedural reasons are **5–003** irrelevant to cases heard in the Employment Tribunal, His Honour Judge Serota held in *De Souza v Vinci Construction UK Ltd* March 2015 EAT, not following two earlier decisions by which he was not bound, that the *Simmons v Castle* 10 per cent uplift has no application in the Employment Tribunal.

(1) *Pain and suffering and loss of amenities*

Add at the end of the paragraph: Although this work treats mental distress **5–004** (below at heading (4)) as a separate head of non-pecuniary loss, there can sometimes be a fine line between an award for suffering and an award for mental distress. In *ABC v WH* [2015] EWHC 2687 QB the third party defendant was found liable for assault and intentional infliction of emotional harm due to his direct physical sexual abuse of the claimant as well as his emotional manipulation of her and encouragement of her to send him indecent images. The claimant suffered serious distress, including making more than one attempt on her life and injuring herself. The trial judge awarded damages of £25,000, for "pain, suffering and loss of amenity" but it is clear that these damages also included a component for mental distress.

NOTE 18: Insert before the last sentence of the note: And the Supreme Court **5–007** in *Rhodes v OPO (by his litigation friend BHM)* [2015] UKSC 32, reversing the

Court of Appeal, held that *Wilkinson v Downton* did not apply in relation to the publication of an autobiographical book by a father which might lead to his child's psychiatric illness.

(4) *Mental distress*

5–012   Insert a new note before "the mental anxiety" on the last line but two of the paragraph:

NOTE 40a: *Rothwell* has been statutorily reversed in both Scotland and Northern Ireland, each enacting that asbestos-related pleural plaques shall constitute an actionable personal injury: see, respectively, Damages (Asbestos-related Conditions) (Scotland) Act 2009 and Damages (Asbestos-related Conditions) Act (Northern Ireland) 2011. *McCauley v Harland & Wolff Plc* [2014] NIQB 91 is a Northern Ireland damages case following upon the statutory reversal.

5–013   Add at the end of the paragraph: Another example is the tort of intentional infliction of emotional harm. In *ABC v WH* [2015] EWHC 2687 QB (above) damages for the tort of intentional infliction of emotional harm were awarded for "pain, suffering and loss of amenity", including a component for mental distress.

II. CONTRACT

5–016   NOTE 63: Add at the end of the note: Since these procedural reasons are irrelevant to cases heard in the Employment Tribunal, His Honour Judge Serota held in *De Souza v Vinci Construction UK Ltd* March 2015 EAT, not following two earlier decisions by which he was not bound, that the *Simmons v Castle* 10 per cent uplift has no application in the Employment Tribunal.

BOOK ONE

PART THREE

THE LIMITS OF COMPENSATORY DAMAGES

CHAPTER 7

REDUCTION OF DAMAGES FOR CONTRIBUTORY NEGLIGENCE

1. Liability in Tort

(2) *Apportionment*

Insert a new paragraph after para.7–006:

That the decision on apportionment is so much a matter of impression is **7–006A** dramatically illustrated by *Jackson v Murray* [2015] UKSC 5, a case from Scotland of a child running into the path of an oncoming vehicle, a not unfamiliar story in the annals of contributory negligence. Not only was the trial judge's reduction of the 13-year-old girl's damages by 90 per cent changed down by the Scots appeal court to 70 per cent and further changed down by the Supreme Court to 50 per cent but also the reduction by the Supreme Court was only by a bare majority, the minority agreeing with the Scots appeal court's 70 per cent. Reference was made to the potentially dangerous nature of driving a car, which could do much more damage to a person than a person was likely to do to a car. And it was agreed that an appeal court could only interfere with an apportionment made if it could be said that it lay outside the generous ambit within which reasonable disagreement was possible. Clearly, however, different views were taken as to whether here this generous ambit had or had not been crossed. The majority speech and the minority one are both worth perusal. This guidance of the Supreme Court Justices in *Jackson* on the correct approach of an appellate court to apportionment in contributory negligence has since been adopted by the Court of Appeal in *McCracken v Smith* [2015] EWCA Civ 380, where there had been a collision between a minibus and a trial bike being recklessly and illegally driven. It was again held, though here unanimously, that the generous ambit within which reasonable disagreement was possible had been crossed, and the court increased, rather than reduced, the trial judge's 30 per cent attributed to the claimant, the bike's pillion rider, to 50 per cent (together with an agreed 15 per cent on account of the claimant's not wearing a crash helmet).

7–007   NOTE 22: Add at the end of the note: In *Blackmore v Department of Communities and Local Government* Unreported 23 October 2014 County Court, where the cause of an employee's injury and subsequent death was by the combined effect of his smoking and his exposure to asbestos by his employers, the trial judge held that he need not base the deduction for contributory negligence on a mathematical calculation of relative contribution to risk. Instead he considered that the employers should bear the lion's share of responsibility on account of their prolonged breaches of statutory duty and, while the risk from the employee's smoking was probably twice or thrice the risk from the employers' asbestos, he assessed the contributory negligence at 30 per cent.

CHAPTER 8

REMOTENESS OF DAMAGE

I. TORT

(A) *CAUSATION*

2. CAUSE IN FACT: THE NORM AND THE EXCEPTIONS

(2) *The exceptions*

8–019   Insert a new note at the end of the paragraph:

NOTE 54a: It was held in *Heneghan v Manchester Dry Docks Ltd* [2016] EWCA Civ 86 that *Fairchild*, together with the related *Barker v Corus*, applied as much to the contraction of lung cancer as to the contraction of mesothelioma. See the case at para.8–021B, below.

Insert two new paragraphs after para.8–021:

8–021A   The very exceptional nature of the causation test in *Fairchild* was confirmed in *International Energy Group Ltd v Zurich Insurance Plc UK* [2015] UKSC 33, [2015] 2 W.L.R. 1471. The claimant employer exposed an employee to asbestos dust over 27 years of employment. The employee contracted mesothelioma. The employee compromised his claim with his employer and the employer sought an indemnity from its insurer. The insurer had provided cover for six of the 27 years of employment for injuries or disease "caused during any period of insurance and arising out of . . . his employment". As the claim was governed by the laws of Guernsey, the Compensation Act 2006 did not apply. Much of the decision turned upon principles concerning contribution between the insurer and the employer and other insurers who were liable for other years of the 27-year period. However, the importance of the decision for the purpose of causation is in relation to the regrets expressed by their Lordships at having departed from the "but for" test for causation and the manner in which the *Fairchild* exception would be confined. In the majority, Lord Mance (with whom Lords Clarke, Carnwath and Hodge agreed) spoke of the rule in *Fairchild* as an "exceptional basis of a weak or broad causal link consisting of exposure to a risk" ([39]). Lord Hodge, in a concurring judgment, said that the case was an example of how the courts have continued to grapple with the consequences of departing from the "but for" test of causation ([98]). In the minority, Lord Sumption (with whom Lord Neuberger and Lord Reed agreed) also expressed some regret about the decision in *Fairchild*. His Lordship referred to the post-retirement lament of Lord Hoffmann that the House of Lords in *Fairchild* did not perform its ordinary function of changing the common law to modify some principle that is found to be unsatisfactory. Instead, a special exception was created "which could not be justified by reference to any general principle and depended on a distinction which had no rational factual or legal justification" ([128]). Although the rule cannot rationally be confined only to mesothelioma, the causal principle described by their Lordships as the "*Fairchild* enclave" is likely to be confined, as Lords Neuberger and Reed said, to a "disease which has the unusual features of mesothelioma" ([191]).

The contours of the *Fairchild* enclave were considered in *Reaney v University* **8–021B** *Hospital of North Staffordshire NHS Trust* [2015] EWCA Civ 1119. In that case, the Court of Appeal confirmed that although no distinction could be drawn between cases of medical negligence and others, the "but for" test for causation was only to be displaced in cases where there is a material contribution, and there are gaps in medical science. The Master of the Rolls, Lord Dyson, with whom Tomlinson and Lewison LJJ agreed, at [35] approved the statement from *Bailey v Ministry of Defence* [2009] 1 W.L.R. 1052, 1069 [46]:

> "In my view one cannot draw a distinction between medical negligence cases and others. I would summarise the position in relation to cumulative cause cases as follows. If the evidence demonstrates on a balance of probabilities that the injury would have occurred as a result of the non-tortious cause or causes in any event, the claimant will have failed to establish that the tortious cause contributed. *Hotson's* case exemplifies such a situation. If the evidence demonstrates that 'but for' the contribution of the tortious cause the injury would probably not have occurred, the claimant will (obviously) have discharged the burden. In a case where medical science cannot establish the probability that 'but for' an act of negligence the injury would not have happened but can establish that the contribution of the negligent cause was more than negligible, the 'but for' test is modified, and the claimant will succeed."

This statement suggests that cases of "material contribution" are an exception to the "but for" test where the negligence was not necessary for the loss but merely contributed to loss that would have occurred anyway. As we saw above, a similar statement was made by Lord Rodger in *Fairchild* [2003] 1 A.C. 32 [129].

The suggestion in *Bailey* that "material contribution" should be given a meaning which creates an alternative test for causation was rejected by the Privy Council in *Williams v The Bermuda Hospitals Board (Bermuda)* [2016] UKPC 4. Mr Williams had acute appendicitis but the hospital he attended delayed his treatment and appendectomy. He suffered loss because he was seriously unwell for several weeks with complications including sepsis. The sepsis had already begun to develop but the hospital's delay exacerbated the development of it. One question was whether the culpable delay had caused the loss suffered. Lord Toulson, giving the advice of the Privy Council, held that the delay had caused the complications. The central argument concerned the meaning of the decision in *Bonnington*. The Privy Council, at [32], emphasised that the House of Lords in *Bonnington* had assumed that the pneumoconiosis was a cumulative injury *not* a divisible injury. Hence the "guilty dust" had increased the severity of the injury. Further, *Bonnington* was concerned with liability, not quantum. There was no submission that the quantum should be limited to the amount by which the injury had been increased by the guilty dust. In other words, the "material contribution" of the guilty dust in *Bonnington* was still a "but for" cause of the loss because the loss, in its totality, would not have occurred without the guilty dust. For this reason, the Privy Council, at [47], held that the Court of Appeal in *Bailey* was incorrect to suggest that the material contribution test in *Bonnington*, "involved a departure from the 'but-for' test". The Privy Council in *Williams* also rejected the submission that the material contribution approach in *Bonnington* was confined to cases where the sources of the loss were simultaneous (the guilty dust and the innocent dust). However, at [39], the Privy Council said that the sequence of events might still be relevant to determine whether an earlier event had been so overtaken by later events that it was not a material contribution to the outcome.

Unfortunately, without reference to *Williams,* in *Heneghan v Manchester Dry Docks Ltd* [2016] EWCA Civ 86 the Court of Appeal returned to the earlier understanding of "material contribution". In that case, Mr Heneghan died of lung cancer caused by his exposure to asbestos fibres whilst he was employed successively by each of the six defendants. His son could not prove by biological evidence which exposure had led to the cell changes that caused the disease. However, counsel argued that statistical evidence could prove how much each defendant had increased the risk of the disease. The Court of Appeal applied the *Fairchild* exception, as developed in *Barker v Corus UK Ltd* [2006] UKHL 20, [2006] 2 A.C. 572. There was a compelling case to do so, especially since the Court of Appeal held that the circumstances were not materially different from *Fairchild.* However, at [23] the Master of the Rolls, with whom Tomlinson and Sales LJJ agreed, said that there are three ways of proving causation in disease cases: (1) by showing that "but for" the defendant's negligence, the claimant would not have suffered the disease; (2) by showing that the disease is caused by the cumulative effect of an agency, part of which is attributable to breach of duty on the part of the defendant which made a "material contribution" to the *injury*; and (3) by showing that the disease is indivisible (such as mesothelioma) and the defendant materially increased the *risk* of the victim contracting the disease: the *Fairchild* exception. Mr Heneghan succeeded only on category (3) for the increased *risk* of injury and hence he could not recover the full amount of damages for a material contribution to an *injury* (category (2)). Nevertheless, category (2) has the potential to confuse by suggesting, contrary to the decision in *Williams,* that material contribution is an alternative to "but for" causation.

The two decisions in *Williams* and *Heneghan* were confronted by Picken J in *John v Central Manchester and Manchester Children's University Hospitals NHS Foundation Trust* [2016] EWHC 407 QB. That case involved the defendant hospital's negligence in delaying a CT scan of Dr John's brain after an accident. Dr John suffered a brain injury from his accident which was exacerbated by a post-operative infection. However, a further factor was the hospital's delay. If Dr

John's CT scan had not been delayed by an hour, he would have been operated upon an hour earlier and he would have avoided a period of raised intra-cranial pressure for an hour. The primary judge considered the three categories from *Heneghan,* as he was required to do, and held that since Dr John's case was not an industrial disease case, it was not concerned with contribution to *risk* (category (3)). He treated it as concerned with material contribution to *injury* or *damage* (category (2)). He concluded that since the material contribution test applied to multi-factor cases as well as single factor cases, full damages should be recovered, without apportionment for the extent to which any other cause contributed to the injury. In other words, Dr John recovered not merely for the amount by which the delay *increased* his injury. He recovered for the whole of the injury. The primary judge held, at [98], that if the "material contribution" test is satisfied, then causation is made out and the entirety of the loss can be recovered if it is not possible to attribute particular damage to a specific cause. The difficulty with this conclusion is that it conflates two different concepts. The material contribution is to the *injury* but the *loss* which has been caused is the *increase* or *exacerbation* of the injury. In other words, the brain injury would have occurred even without the hospital's negligence but the increase in the injury from the material contribution would not. Unless causation is confined in this way, the material contribution test would genuinely be a new test for causation separate from the "but for" test.

4. Cause in Law: Consequences Following Upon a New Intervening Force

(2) *Intervening acts of the claimant*

NOTE 298: Add at the end of the note: *McCracken v Smith* [2015] EWCA Civ 380 (at para.7–006A, above) is a further case where *ex turpi causa* and contributory negligence are intertwined. **8–063**

(B) *SCOPE OF PROTECTION: THE LIMITS OF POLICY*

2. Foreseeable Damage Caused in an Unforeseeable Manner or to an Unforeseeable Degree Where a Breach of a Duty to the Claimant to Take Care Has Been Established

(1) *Direct consequences*

NOTE 448 to be deleted. **8–090**

4. Damage Outside the Scope of the Duty

Add at the end of the paragraph: From exposure to platinum salts in their employment, the five claimants in *Greenway v Johnson Matthey Plc* [2014] **8–134**

EWHC 3957 QB developed sensitivity to platinum. While this sensitisation did not produce physical or physiological harm to them, it prevented their continuing in their work involving contact with platinum. It was held, applying SAAMCO, that the scope of the employer's statutory duty lay in the safeguarding of its employees from the risk of personal harm and the claimants were therefore debarred from suing for their economic loss: see *ibid.* at [34].

II. CONTRACT

(A) *CAUSATION*

2. CONSEQUENCES FOLLOWING UPON A NEW INTERVENING FORCE

(2) *Intervening acts of the claimant*

8–147   Insert a new note at the end of the paragraph:

NOTE 746a: The Court of Appeal in *Stacey v Autosleeper Group Ltd* [2014] EWCA Civ 1551 relied on both the *Girocentrale* and the *Borealis* cases to hold that the buyer of a motor home was entitled to damages for breach of warranty for his loss, by way of costs of litigation with his sub-buyer, as his failure to notice the inconsistency between the gross weight stamped on the chassis plate and the greater gross weight warranted was not reckless.

(B) *SCOPE OF PROTECTION: CONTEMPLATION OF THE PARTIES*

8–156   NOTE 781: Add at the end of the note: The liability of the employer in *Greenway v Johnson Matthey Plc* [2014] EWHC 3957 QB, considered at para.8–134, above, was in breach of contract as well as in tort for breach of statutory duty. The result was the same. The employer's duty, operating through an implied term imposed by the law, was to maintain a safe place of work and to care for the physical safety of employees; thus the implied term was exactly co-extensive with the tortious obligation. So in contract as in tort the scope of the duty did not go beyond physical injury to reach economic loss: see *ibid.* at [43]–[47].

4. THE IMPACT OF THE DECISION IN *THE ACHILLEAS* IN 2008

(2) *The aftermath of the decision*

8–177   Insert a new note at the end of the first sentence:

NOTE 859a: A further case in which *The Achilleas* and the assumption of responsibility test was held to have no application is *Saipol SA v Inerco Trade SA*

[2014] EWHC 2211 (Comm) where there was a sale of sunflower seed oil contaminated in the shipping of it: see *ibid.* at [15]–[18]. Also in *SC Confectia SA v Miss Mania Wholesale Ltd* [2014] EWCA Civ 1484, where there was a sale of defective garments, the Court of Appeal held *The Achilleas* to have no possible application: see *ibid.* at [15], [24]–[26].

MITIGATION OF DAMAGE

In the table of contents for Chapter 9, heading IV, replace the words "which the claimant has avoiided" with "which the claimant has avoided".

I. VARIOUS MEANINGS OF THE TERM "MITIGATION"

1. PRINCIPAL MEANING: THE THREE RULES AS TO THE AVOIDING OF THE CONSEQUENCES OF A WRONG

Insert a new paragraph after para.9–006:

9–006A   These three rules were endorsed in *Fulton Shipping Inc of Panama v Globalia Business Travel SAU* [2015] EWCA Civ 1299 [14] and again in *Thai Airways International Public Co Ltd v KI Holdings Co Ltd* [2015] EWHC 1250 (Comm). In the latter case, Thai Airways claimed damages from KI Holdings for breaches of contract in relation to the supply of economy class aircraft seats. Some seats were delivered late and others were not delivered. Thai Airways was prevented from using five of its aircraft for 18 months pending the delivery of the seats from another supplier. The issue at trial was whether Thai Airways had mitigated its loss. Leggatt J endorsed these three different rules for mitigation (see [32]), although suggesting that the three rules had an underlying unity based on causation. With respect, the underlying unity does not lie in the notion of causation but, as Leggatt J recognised at [33], the unity lies in a rule that damages are assessed as if the claimant acted reasonably, if in fact it did not act reasonably: quoting A. Dyson and A. Kramer, "There is No 'Breach Date Rule'" (2014) 130 LQR 259 at 263.

The discussion in the paragraphs that follow is consistent with the observation by Leggatt J that the concept of acting reasonably can be deconstructed into various norms of reasonable conduct including the dominant norm that it is reasonable for a claimant to enter an available market as soon as possible to obtain a substitute for a defendant's performance.

2. THE TWO SUBSIDIARY OR RESIDUAL MEANINGS

9–009   NOTE 3: Add at the end of the note: The use of the term "aggravated damage" also avoids confusing statements such as that aggravated *damages* "are only to be awarded where the compensation element is not in itself sufficient to properly compensate": *ABC v WH* [2015] EWHC 2687 QB [104] where compensation was sufficient to "compensate" for the extreme breaches of trust and abuse by the third party.

II. THE RULE AS TO AVOIDABLE LOSS: NO RECOVERY FOR LOSS WHICH THE CLAIMANT OUGHT TO HAVE AVOIDED

1. VARIOUS ASPECTS OF THE RULE

9–017   **(c) The question of duty.** Add at the end of the paragraph: The point was recently reiterated by Lord Toulson (with whom Lord Neuberger, Lord Mance and Lord Clarke agreed) in *Bunge SA v Nidera BV* [2015] UKSC 43 at [81]:

II. The Rule as to Avoidable Loss

"the so-called duty to mitigate is not a duty in the sense that the innocent party owes an obligation to the guilty party to do so (*Darbishire v Warran* [1963] 1 W.L.R. 1067, 1075, per Pearson LJ)."

NOTE 40: Add at the end of the note: See also *Bunge SA v Nidera BV* [2015] **9–018** UKSC 43 at [81] per Lord Toulson.

Insert new paragraphs after para.9–030:

White and Carter v McGregor [1962] A.C. 413 (at para.9–023 of the main **9–030A** text) has made a further appearance, being applied in *MSC Mediterranean Shipping Co SA v Cottonex Anstalt* [2016] EWCA Civ 789. The Swiss seller of a large consignment of raw cotton to a purchaser in Bangladesh contracted to have it shipped by a carrier in 35 of the carrier's sea containers. The contract of carriage provided that for 14 days after the discharge of the cargo in the containers the shipper was entitled to retain the containers without charge. After expiry of those 14 days the shipper was required to pay container demurrage (see para.15–073, below) at a specified daily rate until the containers were returned. The provision was completely open-ended so that it appeared that payment of demurrage could continue indefinitely.

The market for raw cotton collapsed shortly after the conclusion of the contract **9–030B** of sale. So the purchaser sought to escape from the contract and did not collect the cotton. A dispute ensued but the purchaser eventually agreed to pay. On 27 September 2011, the shipper informed the carrier that it no longer had title to the containers. On 2 February 2012, the carrier offered to sell the containers to the shipper but no agreement could be reached. In commercial terms the containers had then been lost. The cotton remained in the containers until the time of the trial.

The Court of Appeal held that the carrier did not have a legitimate interest to **9–030C** refuse to accept the breach after 2 February 2012. The decision of the primary judge, Leggatt J, had been that the legitimate interest ceased on 27 September 2011. The Court of Appeal disagreed, finding that the commercial purpose of the agreement only failed on 2 February 2012 so that the *White and Carter* principle did not apply from that date. After that date the carrier was suffering no loss and was keeping the contract alive merely in order to claim demurrage indefinitely. Referring to *Geys v Société Générale* [2013] 1 A.C. 523, Moore-Bick LJ (with whom Tomlinson LJ and Keehan J agreed) said (at [40]) that the true explanation of the legitimate interest restriction may be that in an appropriate case the court in the exercise of its general equitable jurisdiction will decline to grant the innocent party the remedy to which he or she would normally be entitled. The issue was one of legitimate interest, not mitigation ([49]–[50]).

3. ILLUSTRATIONS OF CIRCUMSTANCES RAISING THE ISSUE OF WHETHER LOSS
SHOULD HAVE BEEN AVOIDED

(1) *Contract*

9–044   *(i) Sale of goods.* NOTE 172: Add at the end of the note: In *SC Confectia SA v Miss Mania Wholesale Ltd* [2014] EWCA Civ 1484 there was a sale of defective garments which the buyer sold on and, on discovery of the defects, wished to retrieve the garments from its sub-buyer but could not do so as the sub-buyer had gone into liquidation. The Court of Appeal held that there was no failure to mitigate, but the one reasoned judgement is not thought to be too clear either on mitigation or, for the purpose of damages, on the correct valuation of the garments.

9–046   *(iii) Contracts for professional services: surveyors, valuers and solicitors.* Add at the end of the paragraph: Negligent advice causing losses can also lead to a reduction in liability if the client fails to mitigate the loss. *LSREF III Wight Ltd v Gateley LLP* [2016] EWCA Civ 359 involved negligence by a firm of solicitors who had been retained by a bank to provide advice in relation to property being offered as security for a loan. The negligence was a failure to advise about an insolvency forfeiture clause in a lease over the property. The security was worth £240,000 less than it would have been if the clause had not been present. Prior to the trial, the lessor offered to remove the clause for £150,000. The solicitors offered to pay this. But the bank (by its assignee) refused this offer. The solicitors alleged that the bank (or its assignee) had failed to mitigate its loss. The Court of Appeal accepted this submission and held that the loss was suffered at the time of entry into the transaction. Simply because the security has not been realised did not prevent the loss being suffered, as measured by the difference in value between the security with the clause and the security without the clause. Realisation of the security would simply crystallise that loss. The bank had unreasonably failed to mitigate that loss by failing to accept the lessor's offer to vary the lease.

IV. THE RULE AS TO AVOIDED LOSS: NO RECOVERY FOR LOSS
WHICH THE CLAIMANT HAS AVOIDED, UNLESS THE MATTER IS
COLLATERAL

3. ACTIONS TAKEN AFTER THE WRONG BY THE CLAIMANT

9–115   Add at the end of the paragraph: Put in longer terms, as recent cases have expressed this point, "if a claimant adopts by way of mitigation a measure which arises out of the consequences of the breach and is in the ordinary course of business and such measure benefits the claimant, that benefit is normally to be brought into account in assessing the claimant's loss unless the measure is wholly independent of the relationship of the claimant and the defendant": *Bacciottini & anor v Gotelee and Goldsmith (A Firm)* [2016] EWCA Civ 170 [49] (Davis LJ); *Fulton Shipping Inc of Panama v Globalia Business Travel SAU ("The New Flamenco")* [2015] EWCA Civ 1299 [23] (Longmore LJ).

(1) *Situations where the benefit is generally taken into account*

Add at the end of the paragraph: In *Bacciottini & anor v Gotelee and* **9–122** *Goldsmith (A Firm)* [2016] EWCA Civ 170 the appellants purchased a property for development. They would not have purchased the property but for negligent advice from their solicitors who failed to inform them that the property was subject to a planning restriction. The appellants subsequently had the restriction removed. They sought damages for the negligence of their solicitors of £100,000 as the difference in value due to the presence of the planning restriction. The Court of Appeal affirmed the decision of the primary judge for damages of £250, representing the cost of the application to the local authority to remove the planning restriction. The Court of Appeal (Davis LJ; Lloyd Jones and Underhill LJJ agreeing) held that, irrespective of whether the appellants were under a duty to mitigate their losses, the reality was that they took the step of applying to remove the restriction, and avoided their putative loss.

(2) *Situations where the benefit is generally ignored*

Insert a new paragraph after para.9–135:

In *Fulton Shipping Inc of Panama v Globalia Business Travel SAU ("The New* **9–135A** *Flamenco")* [2015] EWCA Civ 1299, the Court of Appeal considered the damages arising from early redelivery under a time charterparty. The charter still had two years to run but there was no available market on redelivery. So the owners decided to sell the vessel. They sold it for $16.76 million more than they would have obtained if the vessel had been sold at the end of the charter. The marine arbitrator held that this benefit should be taken into account in calculating the damages. The primary judge, Popplewell J, at [2015] 1 All E.R. Comm 1205, held that it should not. His principal reason was because the decision to sell had not been caused by the breach. But the Court of Appeal held that it should be taken into account, applying *The Kildare* and *The Wren* (*Zodiac Maritime Agencies Ltd v Fortescue Metals Group Ltd ("The Kildare")* [2011] 2 Lloyd's Rep. 360; *Glory Wealth Shipping Pte. Ltd v Korea line Corporation ("The Wren")* [2011] 2 Lloyd's Rep. 370).

In the leading judgment in the Court of Appeal, Longmore LJ distinguished *The Elena D'Amico* [1980] 1 Lloyd's Rep. 75. In that case, Robert Goff J held that if the innocent party chooses to speculate as to the way in which the market is going to go, the result of such speculation is for his account not the account of the guilty party. At [35], Longmore LJ said that this reasoning "all depends on there being an available market which the innocent party decides for reasons of his own to ignore". But where there is no available market, the prima facie measure of loss is not the difference between the contractual hire and the cost of earning that hire if the shipowner is able to mitigate the loss by trading his vessel. If he does so trade the vessel, he may make additional losses or additional profits but, in either event, they should be taken into account. He is not speculating on the market as he would be if there was an available market of which he chooses not to avail himself. At [38], Longmore LJ approved the remarks of Leggatt J in *Thai Airways International Public Co Ltd v KI Holdings Co Ltd* [2015] EWHC 1250 (Comm) [176] that "when the defendant's breach of contract combines with another effective cause to result in loss to the claimant, the loss is recoverable . . . the same principle must apply to gains."

4. ACTIONS TAKEN AFTER THE WRONG BY THIRD PARTIES

(3) *Miscellaneous situations*

Insert a new paragraph after para.9–155:

9–155A   In *Swynson Ltd v Lowick Rose LLP* [2015] EWCA Civ 629, a firm of accountants negligently, in breach of contract, failed to exercise care in a due diligence report into a prospective borrower. The lending company lent money in 2006 and 2007 to the borrower in reliance upon this report. The owner of the lending company lent money to the borrower in 2008. When the borrower was in severe financial distress, the owner of the lending company repaid the 2006 and 2007 loans for various commercial reasons. The accountants argued that they could not be liable for the 2006 and 2007 loans because these were losses that had not been suffered; the loans had been repaid. A majority of the Court of Appeal (Longmore and Sales LJJ) held that the loss had not been avoided by mitigation because the repayment by the owner was a collateral matter, equivalent to an act of benevolence, which should be disregarded when determining loss. Nor had the loss been avoided because it arose "out of the consequences of the defendant's breach of duty and in the ordinary course of business" (at [17]). The decision of Stephenson LJ in *London and South of England Building Society v Stone* [1983] 1 W.L.R. 1424 was confined to cases involving the ordinary course of business. Davis LJ dissented, explaining that the owner's decision was wholly commercial and further that the decision was made to lend money to a separate company which then repaid the borrowing company. The intermediate company was not the owner and the corporate veil could not be lifted.

CHAPTER 10

CERTAINTY OF DAMAGE

In the table of contents for Chapter 10, heading II, replace the words "the natue of the damage" with "the nature of the damage".

I. THE PROBLEM OF CERTAINTY

Remove NOTE 26 in para.10–006.

Add at the end of the paragraph: On one view, the *Armory* principle was **10–006** expanded by the Court of Appeal in *Representative Claimants (Gulati) v MGN Ltd* [2015] EWCA Civ 1291 [107] where the Court of Appeal upheld sizeable awards for phone hacking despite the absence in some cases of any records detailing the hacking and other wrongful activities. In the judgment with which the other judges agreed, Arden LJ said that the award of damages was "an example of the ability of the law to prevent a person responsible for wrongdoing from escaping liability to his victim, without disturbing the general rule as to the conditions of liability". On an expansive view, Arden LJ might be read as suggesting that a claim can be brought for loss caused by hacking against a proved hacker without proving any of the instances of hacking. This cannot be what Arden LJ meant. Her remarks are better understood as suggesting that in all of the circumstances of that case, inferences can be drawn of the nature and extent of the hacking which occurred based on the extent of the related wrongdoing by MGN.

II. CIRCUMSTANCES IN WHICH DAMAGES MAY BE AWARDED ALTHOUGH THE NATURE OF THE DAMAGE PREVENTS ABSOLUTE CERTAINTY OF PROOF

3. WHERE IT IS UNCERTAIN HOW A PECUNIARY LOSS IS TO BE MEASURED

10–012   Insert a new note after the first sentence of the paragraph:

NOTE 39a: In assessing the uncertain loss of profits arising from a supplier's breach of an exclusive supply agreement in *Globe Motors Inc v TRW Lucas Varity Electric Steering Ltd* [2015] EWHC 553 (Comm), the judge had little alternative, after very lengthy submissions by both sides on the calculation of the damages, to taking a broad brush approach.

10–013   NOTE 44: Add at the end of the note: The application of the reflective loss principle in relation to damages is further discussed in the factual context of *Malhotra v Malhotra* [2014] EWHC 113 (Comm) at [53]–[63], *Energenics Holdings Pte Ltd v Ronendra Nath Hazarika* [2014] EWHC 1845 Ch at [60]–[70], and *Barnett v Creggy* [2014] EWHC 3080 Ch at [92]–[99].

4. WHERE IT IS UNCERTAIN HOW MUCH OF THE LOSS, PECUNIARY OR NON-PECUNIARY, IS ATTRIBUTABLE TO THE DEFENDANT'S BREACH OF DUTY

10–021   Insert a new note at the end of the paragraph:

NOTE 84a: *Heneghan v Manchester Dry Docks Ltd* [2014] EWHC 4190 QB was a claim brought on account of the death from lung cancer of a smoker who had been exposed to asbestos during his working life. The defendants were six of his employers over a period of some 10 years; earlier employers were not sued. It was agreed between the parties that the share of the deceased's exposure to asbestos attributable to the six employers sued was some 35 per cent; also agreed was the distribution of the exposures between the six. It was agreed by the medical experts that on the balance of probabilities it was the exposure to asbestos and not the smoking that caused the death. The issue to be decided was whether the defendants were each liable for the whole of the damage caused or for only the 35 per cent. In a long, complex judgment, Jay J decided for the 35 per cent, applying the *Fairchild* principle together with the apportionment ruling in *Barker v Corus*.

In contrast, Jay J refused to award damages in *Saunderson v Sonae Industria (UK) Ltd* [2015] EWHC 2264 QB. In that case, group litigation was brought by thousands of claimants for personal injuries arising from negligence and public nuisance when fire broke out at the defendant's chemical plant in Kirkby. The plant was near the claimants' homes or workplaces. The claimants failed to establish liability. At [186], Jay J explained that the *Fairchild* principle meant that it was incumbent on the claimants to prove on the balance of probabilities that they were within the relevant envelope of material risk as that concept is properly understood. It is insufficient that there was a risk in the sense that the claimants had *some* exposure such as a minuscule exposure, measurable only in parts per trillion. The exposure must be at a level that was capable of causing personal injury.

Insert a new paragraph after para.10–026:

The rule that seems to have settled, as affirmed in *Reaney v University*   **10–026A**
Hospital of North Staffordshire NHS Trust & Anor [2015] EWCA Civ 1119 [35] is that the "but for" test for causation is displaced only in cases where there is a material contribution and there are gaps in medical science.

5. Where it is Uncertain whether a Particular Pecuniary Loss will be or would have been Incurred

(4) *Loss of a chance*

Insert a new paragraph after para.10–049:

(iia) The need to prove a real and substantial chance. In *Harding Homes (East* **10–049A**
Street) Ltd & Ors v Bircham Dyson Bell (a firm) [2015] EWHC 3329 (Ch), the defendant solicitors were negligent by including an all monies clause in a guarantee given by the claimant builders to a bank in relation to a property development. The guarantee should have been limited to interest shortfall and cost overruns. The claimants alleged that they lost the opportunity for a more profitable result arising from negotiations about the development with the bank.

The trial judge, Proudman J, considered whether the loss of opportunity was of something of value; that is, something that had a real and substantial rather than a merely negligible prospect of success. In concluding that prospects of success were negligible, the trial judge, at [167], followed *Thomas v Albutt*

[2015] EWHC 2817 (Ch) at [461] where Morgan J said that if "the prospects were 10 per cent or less, then I should regard them as negligible". It is difficult to justify such mathematical precision in relation to a broadly expressed approach to "negligible" prospects of success. But even if this point were to be expressed in mathematical terms, the better approach is that a "negligible" prospect should be assessed in light of the circumstances. For instance, a 10 per cent prospect of succeeding in relation to a transaction worth billions of pounds might not be negligible for the same company compared with one which is worth thousands.

10–065   Add at the end of the paragraph: The principle that hypothetical actions of third parties are assessed on the basis of a need to prove a "substantial chance" but that a claimant's hypothetical actions must be proved on the balance of probabilities was confirmed in *Wellesley Partners LLP v Withers LLP* [2015] EWCA Civ 1146. In that case, Floyd LJ, in the leading judgment on this issue, set out his basic understanding of the position before undertaking a comprehensive examination of the authorities to confirm that it was correct. His Lordship said that the claimant head-hunters (WP) needed to prove their actions on the balance of probabilities but only a real and substantial chance of benefit from the actions of the third party (Nomura). His Lordship said (at [100]):

> "I would have thought that, applying those principles to the present case, it would be plain that, whilst WP would need to show on the balance of probabilities that, but for the negligence complained of, they would have opened a US office (a question of causation dependent on what the claimant would have done in the absence of a breach of duty), the actual loss which they claimed to have been caused by the defendant was dependent on the hypothetical actions of a third party, namely Nomura. Accordingly, in line with well-established principle, the chances of Nomura deciding to award the mandates to WP would have to be reflected in the award of damages."

Insert a new paragraph after para.10–066:

10–066A   A significant circumstance where a claim for loss of chance will not succeed is where the claimant cannot prove that the event which might have been profitable would have occurred. In *Wellesley Partners LLP v Withers LLP* [2015] EWCA Civ 1146 a head-hunting firm claimed damages for the loss of a chance of obtaining a profitable contract with an investment bank. The Court of Appeal separated two different enquiries. First, on the balance of probabilities would the headhunters have obtained the contract? Secondly, did they lose a chance of making profit? Consistently with the approach to deny the reduction of damages in cases like *Front Ace* considered in the previous paragraph, the Court of Appeal held that the loss of chance quantification applies only to the latter question.

10–071   Before the final sentence beginning "Further successful loss of chance cases . . . " add: And the claim in *Wellesley Partners LLP v Withers LLP* [2015] EWCA Civ 1146 involved negligence by solicitors which deprived the claimant head-hunting firm of the opportunity of a profitable contract, assessed as a 60 per cent chance.

NOTE 306: Add at end of note: See also *Harding Homes (East Street) Ltd &* **10–073**
Ors v Bircham Dyson Bell (a firm) [2015] EWHC 3329 (Ch).

Insert a new note after the penultimate sentence of the paragraph: **10–083**

NOTE 348a: Also in *Tait v Gloucestershire Hospitals NHS Foundation Trust*
[2015] EWHC 848 QB the *Langford* method is adopted: *ibid.* at [88].

NOTE 381: Add at the end of the note: , where *Hayes v South East Coast* **10–089**
Ambulance Service NHS Foundation Trust [2015] EWHC 18 QB is cited as a
case in which the chance of reconciliation was very high.

(5) *Where certainty is dependent upon the defendant's actions*

NOTE 494: Add at the end of the note: Cases appearing in this section on **10–111**
certainty of loss dependent on the defendant's actions—*Lavarack, Horkulak* and
Durham Tees—come under consideration in *IBM United Kingdom Holdings Ltd*
v Dalgleish [2015] EWHC 389 Ch. See the case at para.31–031 n.185a,
below.

(6) *Where certainty as to the loss suffered is dependent on future events*

Insert a new paragraph after para.10–119:

The Golden Victory [2007] 2 A.C. 353 has of late been much in evidence, on **10–120**
account of contracting parties arguing for the assessment of the damages at a time
after the date of breach of contract because of the future realisation of
contingencies.

Some cases have concerned breach of warranty where shares in a company
have been sold; in all of the cases the argument has failed. The issue received
consideration by Popplewell J in the earliest case, *Ageas (UK) Ltd v Kwik-Fit*
(GB) Ltd [2014] EWHC 2178 QB. The breach of warranty resulted from an
overstatement in the company accounts of revenue and assets by reason of the
bad debts of the company at the time of contracting being understated. By the
time of trial four years later the bad debts had become much less. The level of
bad debt was the future uncertain contingency, which later became certain, upon
which the party in breach relied to reduce, if not eliminate, the damages.
Popplewell J rightly held that *The Golden Victory* was not in point. The measure
of damages fell to be assessed in the usual way at the time that the contract was
made which was also the time of breach. The risk of what would happen to the
bad debt position was effectively transferred to the buyer who was entitled to the

benefit if the company business did well and be subject to the loss if it did badly. The compensatory principle was unoffended and there was no windfall to the buyer: see the discussion from *ibid.* at [29]. Similar is *Hut Group Ltd v Nobahar-Cookson* [2014] EWHC 3842 QB. Neither the assets and liabilities nor the profit and loss of the company had been fairly presented and the question was, once again and with *The Golden Victory* again in mind, the extent to which matters following the breach of warranty could be taken into account in the assessment of the damages. Blair J, who not unreasonably was unclear as to what the future uncertain contingency here comprised, held that such matters were not to be taken into account as, again, the outcome of all contingencies were risks transferred to the buyer which reaped the benefit or suffered the loss depending on how the business did: see the discussion at [212]–[219]. As for the curious case of *Bir Holdings Ltd v Mehta* [2014] EWHC 3903 Ch, where the claim was by the seller of shares on account of its breach of warranty entitling the buyer to retain a substantial part of the purchase price and where *The Golden Victory* was again brought into play, matters following upon the breach were not taken into account in the assessment of damages, although it appears that the case did not involve future uncertain contingencies: see the discussion from [66]–[81].

The issue arose again in the Supreme Court in *Bunge SA v Nidera BV* [2015] UKSC 43. In that case, unlike Hamblen J whose decision is discussed above at para.10–118, the Supreme Court confronted the question of whether *The Golden Victory* should be applied, and whether it was correctly decided. The sellers argued that it was necessary to take account of events occurring after the breach which showed that the same loss would have been suffered even without the repudiation. The buyers' first argument was that, consistently with the view expressed at para.10–118, the majority view in the *Golden Victory* should not apply to a single cargo. The second argument for the buyers was that *The Golden Victory* was wrongly decided. The third argument was that the agreed damages clause had excluded the compensatory principle enunciated in *The Golden Victory*.

As to the first argument, Lord Sumption (with whom Lords Neuberger, Mance and Clarke agreed) said that the dicta from Lord Scott of Foscote in *The Golden Victory* should not be understood as confining the principle to situations involving successive performances. The principle also applied to cases involving a single instance of performance. Cases involving a single instance of performance might be factually different but the compensatory principle applies to them in the same way. Lord Toulson, who also agreed with Lord Sumption, said that there was "no logical foundation" for a distinction between a single instance of performance and successive performances (at [87]).

As to the second argument, Lord Sumption held that the decision in *The Golden Victory* was neither new nor heterodox. His Lordship rejected the clarion call for certainty on the basis that, although important, "it can rarely be thought to justify an award of substantial damages to someone who has not suffered any" (at [23]). Lord Toulson, who also agreed with Lord Sumption, also expressed the view that *The Golden Victory* was correctly decided and consistent with previous case law (at [87]).

As to the third argument, Lord Sumption held that agreed damages clauses were not necessarily to be regarded as a code, and further that there was no presumption that an agreed damages clause was intended to exclude the common law. However, such a damages clause may be assumed, in the absence of clear words, not to have been intended to operate arbitrarily. An arbitrary operation would include one which produced a result unrelated to anything which, by the compensatory principle, the parties could reasonably have expected to approximate to the true loss. In this case, the agreed damages clause was not a complete code and the provision was consistent with the application of the compensatory principle.

At [21], Lord Sumption said:

"The real difference between the majority and the minority turned on the question what was being valued for the purpose assessing damages. The majority were valuing the chartered service that would actually have been performed if the charterparty had not been wrongfully brought to a premature end. On that footing, the notional substitute contract, whenever it was made and at whatever market rate, would have made no difference because it would have been subject to the same war clause as the original contract ... The minority on the other hand considered that one should value not the chartered service which would actually have been performed, but the charterparty itself, assessed at the time that it was terminated, by reference to the terms of a notional substitute concluded as soon as possible after the termination of the original. That would vary, not according to the actual outcome, but according to the outcomes which were perceived as possible or probable at the time that the notional substitute contract was made. The possibility or probability of war would then be factored into the price agreed in the substitute contract."

A similar observation about the basis for the minority decision (concerned with valuing the *contract* itself) was also made by Lord Toulson at [88].

BOOK TWO

NON-COMPENSATORY DAMAGES

CHAPTER 12

NOMINAL DAMAGES

1. CIRCUMSTANCES GIVING RISE TO AN AWARD OF NOMINAL DAMAGES

(1) *Where there is Injuria Sine Damno*

12–002 NOTE 7: add at the end of the note: See also *R (O) v Secretary of State for the Home Department (Bail for Immigration Detainees)* [2016] UKSC 19; [2016] 1 W.L.R. 1717.

NOTE 8: Insert at the end of the cases listed in the opening sentence of the note: and *The Queen (on the application of Mohammed) v The Secretary of State for the Home Department* [2014] EWHC 1898 (Admin).

NOTE 8: Add at the end of the note: A further case is *Bostridge v Oxleas NHS Foundation Trust* [2015] EWCA Civ 79, where the claimant was a mentally disordered patient and the defendant an NHS trust, which had detained the patient unlawfully, rather than the Secretary of State for the Home Department. In *Bostridge* the Court of Appeal held that for a nominal damages award it mattered not that it was not the NHS trust but a third party that could and would have lawfully detained the claimant.

(2) *Where Damage is Shown but its Amount is Not Sufficiently Proved*

12–005 Add at the end of the paragraph: In *Greer v Alstons Engineering Sales and Services Ltd (Trinidad and Tobago)* [2003] UKPC 46, the Privy Council held that the appellants were entitled to a substantial award of damages for loss of use of a backhoe despite the failure of the appellants to prove any actual use of the backhoe. The Privy Council said that although "loss under this head was unquantified, it is the duty of the court to recognise it by an award that is not out of scale". However, the award of $5,000 was not disturbed because, although on the low side, it was not contrary to principle. Another example of the reluctance of courts to award only nominal damages where clear loss had been suffered but where the claimant has not led sufficient evidence of loss is *Karim v Wemyss* [2016] EWCA Civ 27. In that case, Mr Wemyss sold a solicitor's practice to Mr Karim. Mr Wemyss misrepresented the turnover and profit of the business. Mr Wemyss represented that the business had a profit earning capacity of £120,000 but, in fact, it had only a profit earning capacity of £92,000. Mr Karim succeeded in a claim for breach of contract and for deceit. In the Court of Appeal, Lewison LJ (with whom Kitchin and Longmore LJJ agreed) explained that the contractual measure of damages was concerned with the difference between the true value of the business and its value if the warranted information had complied with the warranty. The tortious measure was concerned with the difference between the true value and the price paid. But the primary judge had no evidence of either (i) the true value, or (ii) the value of the business if the warranted information had been true. Both of those depended on the value of the goodwill which required a multiplier to be applied to the profit earning capacity to reflect the future years of profitability. The Court of Appeal, without expert evidence, and in a very rough and ready way, examined the breakdown of the sale price and estimated that the goodwill was a *fraction* of the warranted profit rather than a multiple of it. This might have suggested that there was little reliance on the warranted profit. In any event, the Court of Appeal made an award of damages of only £15,000 for breach of warranty.

2. AMOUNT AWARDED: NOMINAL AND SMALL DAMAGES DISTINGUISHED

In the heading above para.12–006 change the heading number from "1" to "2".

12–006   NOTE 23: Add at the end of the note: £5 as the award reappears in *The Queen (on the application of Mohammed) v The Secretary of State for the Home Department* [2014] EWHC 1898 (Admin).

3. PRACTICAL FUNCTIONS OF NOMINAL DAMAGES

12–009   NOTE 34: Insert after "illustrative" on line two of the note: as is *Bostridge v Oxleas NHS Foundation Trust* [2015] EWCA Civ 79.

EXEMPLARY DAMAGES

II. CASES IN WHICH EXEMPLARY DAMAGES MAY BE AWARDED

2. THE THREE CATEGORIES IN WHICH EXEMPLARY AWARDS ARE POSSIBLE

(1) *First common law category: oppressive, arbitrary or unconstitutional conduct by government servants*

13–018 Add at the end of the paragraph: Exemplary damages have again been awarded against immigration officers in *Patel v Secretary of State for the Home Department* [2014] EWHC 501 (Admin) (see *ibid.* at [343]) to a youngish Indian woman with leave to enter the United Kingdom to visit her family who was treated appallingly by the officers in their attempt to remove her from the country. See the case further at paras 40–015 and 40–025, below.

(2) *Second common law category: conduct calculated to result in profit*

13–025   Insert a new note after the first sentence of the paragraph:

NOTE 135a: Similar is the potential profit to be made by property owners harassing a neighbouring owner into giving up a right of way over their land, as in *Saxton v Bayliss* Unreported 31 January 2014 Central London County Court (facts at para.41–019 n.81, below).

RESTITUTIONARY DAMAGES

In the contents of Chapter 14, section II, under "2. Liability in contract" amend sub-heading (2) so it reads "The various type situations" rather than "The three type situations".

II. CIRCUMSTANCES GIVING RISE TO RESTITUTIONARY DAMAGES

1. Liability in Tort

(3) *Torts affecting the person*

Insert a new paragraph after para.14–020:

A circumstance removed from assault which might be best understood as an **14–020A** award of restitutionary damages is where a substantial award of damages is made for an infringement of privacy but the claimant suffers no distress or other subjective loss nor any financial loss. In *Representative Claimants (Gulati) v MGN Ltd* [2015] EWCA Civ 1291 substantial awards of damages were made against MGN Ltd, the proprietor of the *Daily Mirror, The Sunday People* and *The Sunday Mirror* newspapers for the misuse of private information by "hacking" of telephone messages. The Court of Appeal held that the damages were independent of any distress or financial loss by the claimant and were not made to "vindicate" any right. Instead the award was made "to compensate for the loss or diminution of a right to control formerly private information and for the distress that the respondents could justifiably have felt because their private information had been exploited". The "lost right of control" was not a financial loss, nor was it a subjective loss to the claimant. If the award of damages for the claimant's "lost right to control private information" is to be justified on a basis independently of any loss suffered by the claimant, and not as an award of vindicatory damages, it is best justified as an award of restitutionary damages, representing the benefit that the defendant derived from the wrongdoing.

As Mance LJ said in *Experience Hendrix LLC v PPX Enterprises Inc* [2003] EWCA Civ 323 [26] "the law gives effect to the instinctive reaction that, whether or not the appellant would have been better off if the wrong had not been committed, the wrongdoer ought not *to gain an advantage for free*, and should make some reasonable recompense." Similar sentiments were expressed by the primary judge, Mann J, in *Gulati* who said that "the defendant will have helped itself, over an extended period of time, to large amounts of personal and private information and treated it as its own to deal with as it thought fit" (*Gulati & Ors v MGN Ltd* [2015] EWHC 1482 (Ch) [132]). This also explains why matters such as (i) the scale of the disclosure and (ii) whether the information would have become public anyway are relevant matters (see [46] in the Court of Appeal) in the assessment of the damages for infringement of the right, irrespective of the consequences suffered. Those matters are concerned with the extent of the advantage obtained by the defendants.

2. LIABILITY IN CONTRACT

(2) *The various type situations*

Insert a new paragraph after para.14–038:

14–038A *(iii) Non-compete clauses.* Another example of a breach of a negative stipulation which leads to restitutionary damages is a breach of a non-compete clause. *Garner v One-Step (Support) Ltd* [2016] EWCA Civ 180 involved breaches of non-compete and non-solicitation covenants in the sale of a business providing "supported living" services. The primary judge allowed the claimants to elect for *Wrotham Park* damages instead of damages for financial loss. The appellants argued that *Wrotham Park* damages can only be awarded (i) where the injured party is unable to demonstrate identifiable financial loss and (ii) where to do so is necessary to avoid manifest injustice. The Court of Appeal rejected these submissions. However, some restrictions were placed on the award of *Wrotham Park* damages. Christopher Clarke LJ (with whom Longmore and King LJJ agreed) held that the absence of financial loss was not a precondition for the award of *Wrotham Park* damages ([118]). The ultimate question is whether these damages are a just response and since the just response is, quintessentially, a matter for the judge to decide, in the absence of any error of principle the decision of the primary judge could not be overturned ([121]).

Christopher Clarke LJ saw the remedy as an exceptional form of compensatory award which does not require proof of loss. So did Longmore LJ whose approach also treated the damages as exceptional ([149]). So much can be readily accepted. But it would be unfortunate for damages in a commercial area of law to be treated as based upon little more than a requirement of discretion and "justice". With great respect, this form of damages cannot be a matter of discretion for the primary judge. The difficulty arises because, as Christopher Clarke LJ recognised at [106], the damages were characterised in *WWF* as *both* "a juridically highly similar remedy to the relief" of an account of profits *and* a compensatory remedy. Both of those statements cannot be true. An account of profits requires the calculation and disgorgement of a *defendant's* profits. A compensatory remedy is concerned with a *claimant's* loss. The reason why *Wrotham Park* damages are juridically similar to the account of profits is because they are *not* compensatory for loss. They are restitutionary. However, unlike an account and disgorgement of all actual profits made, they focus on the reasonable value of the benefit immediately received by the defendant.

CHAPTER 15

LIQUIDATED DAMAGES

1. HISTORICAL DEVELOPMENT OF LIQUIDATED DAMAGES AND PENALTIES

(4) *The modern law*

15–008   Add at the end of the paragraph: In the important conjoined appeals in *Cavendish Square Holdings v Makdessi* and *ParkingEye Ltd v Beavis* [2015] UKSC 67 the United Kingdom Supreme Court conducted an extensive review of all of the law and authorities on liquidated damages and penalties. For details of the case, see paras 15–012A to 15–012I, below.

2. NATURE AND EFFECT OF LIQUIDATED DAMAGES AND PENALTIES

Insert new paragraphs after para.15–012:

15–012A   In the conjoined appeals in *Cavendish Square Holdings v Makdessi* and *ParkingEye Ltd v Beavis* [2015] UKSC 67 the United Kingdom Supreme Court revisited the law of penalties concerning provisions which (i) disentitled a party from receiving sums of money which without breach he would have received and (ii) provisions requiring the transfer of property by the party in breach at an undervalue or for no value. The latter type of provision was addressed in a consideration of *Jobson v Johnson* [1989] 1 W.L.R. 1026 CA in the paragraph preceding this one in the main work but which decision, according to Lords Sumption, Neuberger and Carnwath is no longer authoritative as a penalty case but is entirely conventional only if it is reinterpreted as concerned with relief against forfeiture. The approach of Lords Mance, Hodge, Clarke and Toulson was not as sceptical about the correctness of *Jobson* as a penalties case although a majority of the Supreme Court rejected the conclusion in *Jobson* that the court had power to strike down only that part of a penalty clause which was extravagant and unconscionable. Such a partial invalidation of the clause was said to be impermissible because it would rewrite the contract.

15–012B   In the first appeal before the Supreme Court (*Makdessi*), Mr Makdessi and a colleague held shares in a large advertising and marketing company in the Middle East. Mr Makdessi and his colleague agreed to sell shares to a related company to give it a 60 per cent holding. Cavendish Square Holdings was novated to the related company's rights. The purchase price was to be paid in four instalments. The final two payments could only be calculated in the future, being dependent on the amount of the company's future profits very substantially increased to represent a particularly high figure for goodwill so that the total amount payable could amount to just short of $150 million. Mr Makdessi and his colleague were restricted from trading in the same field in 23 specified countries.

Two crucial provisions of the contract were as follows: if Mr Makdessi **15–012C** breached the restrictive covenants then (i) he would not be entitled to receive the final two instalments of the price paid by Cavendish (clause 5.1); (ii) Cavendish would have a call option to buy Mr Makdessi's remaining shares, at a price excluding the value of the goodwill of the business (clause 5.6). Mr Makdessi subsequently breached the restrictive covenants. He argued that clauses 5.1 and 5.6 were unenforceable penalty clauses. The United Kingdom Supreme Court upheld the validity of the clauses.

The second appeal before the Supreme Court (*ParkingEye*) involved parking **15–012D** charges imposed by the claimant company who managed a car park. The car park was intended for motorist customers of a retail store. A parking charge of £85 was imposed on motorists for overstaying the two-hour permitted period of free parking. Motorists who entered the car park and parked their cars contracted to adhere to the parking rules. Mr Beavis overstayed the free period by just short of an hour. He refused to pay the £85 charge. One ground was that he alleged that it was a penalty. A majority of the United Kingdom Supreme Court (Lord Toulson dissenting) upheld the validity of the clause.

The various judgments expressed reasoning concerning the law of penalties in **15–012E** general terms before applying the reasoning to the two appeals. All of the Supreme Court held that the penalties doctrine was only engaged when there had been a breach of contract. A provision, no matter how extreme, which penalised a party could not be a penalty unless it was consequential upon breach. Lord Neuberger and Lord Sumption (with whom Lord Carnwath agreed) explained that this principle, which had been taken for granted as early as 1939 in *Moss Empires Ltd v Olympia (Liverpool) Ltd* [1939] A.C. 544, depended upon a "fundamental difference between a jurisdiction to review the fairness of a contractual obligation and a jurisdiction to regulate the remedy for its breach" ([12]–[13]). Their Lordships rejected the contrary Australian approach as "a radical departure from the previous understanding of the law", as an approach which was "entirely historical" but not consistent with history, as an approach which is difficult to apply to the case to which it is supposedly directed, and as one which does not "address the major legal and commercial implications of transforming a rule for controlling remedies for breach of contract into a jurisdiction to review the content of the substantive obligations which the parties have agreed" (see *Andrews v Australia and New Zealand Banking Group Ltd* (2012) 247 C.L.R. 205).

As to the question of when a clause would be a penalty, the plurality expres- **15–012F** sion of the test was from Lord Neuberger and Lord Sumption (with whom Lord Carnwath and Lord Clarke agreed, and with the substance of which Lord Mance agreed at [152]). The expression by Lords Hodge and Toulson ([255], [294]) was not substantially different. Lords Neuberger and Sumption recognised that a damages clause may properly be justified by considerations other than the desire to recover compensation for a breach if the innocent party has a legitimate interest in performance extending beyond the prospect of pecuniary compensation flowing directly from the breach. They said at [32]:

> "The true test is whether the impugned provision is a secondary obligation which imposes a detriment on the contract-breaker out of all proportion to any legitimate interest of the innocent party in the enforcement of the primary obligation."

15–012G   In summary then, several points can be made about the operation of the law of penalties following this decision:

(1) A clause can only be a penalty if it operates conditionally upon breach of contract, in other words if it is a secondary obligation arising upon breach;

(2) Whether a clause operates conditionally upon a breach of contract is a question of substance, not form, and drafting techniques by the parties may not be effective if the true operation of a clause is that it is conditional upon breach;

(3) A penalty is not confined to the payment of money; it can include the transfer of property but it will not include cases where a proprietary or possessory right is transferred but defeasible upon breach;

(4) The question whether a clause is a penalty must be asked before asking whether relief against forfeiture should be granted. This is because the penalties doctrine operates at the time the clause comes into operation, not at the time of breach. However, it would be foolish not to plead these doctrines as defences in the alternative to a claim for forfeiture;

(5) The test for whether a clause, conditional on breach, is a penalty is whether it imposes a detriment on the contract-breaker out of all proportion to any legitimate interest of the innocent party in the enforcement of the primary obligation;

(6) In applying this test, courts should consider the circumstances in which the contract was made. In a negotiated contract between properly advised parties of comparable bargaining power involves a strong initial presumption that the parties are the best judges of what is legitimate in a provision dealing with the consequences of breach; and

(7) Once a clause is recognised as a penalty then the consequences are that it is void. There is no power for the court partially to enforce the clause to the extent that it might not have been penal, or to enforce it only on terms. To do so would be to rewrite the contract.

15–012H   Applying the law to the facts of *Makdessi*, the Supreme Court unanimously held that neither clause 5.1 nor clause 5.6 was a penalty. As to whether the clause was a secondary obligation which was conditional upon breach, contrary to the press release issued by the Supreme Court, the view on this issue of Lords Neuberger, Sumption and Carnwath was not a majority finding. Their Lordships held that on their proper construction neither clause was a secondary obligation which was conditional upon breach. Both clause 5.1 and clause 5.6 were, in reality, price adjustment clauses which were primary obligations even if the trigger for the price adjustment was a breach. They were not secondary obligations conditional upon breach. None of the other justices reached this conclusion although Lord Hodge and Lord Clarke considered that there was a "strong argument" that clause 5.1 was a primary obligation. Nevertheless, all of the remaining justices held that these clauses were not penalties because they were not out of proportion to the legitimate interest to be protected.

Applying the law to the facts of *ParkingEye*, all of the court held that the parking charge was conditional upon breach. However, eight justices (Lord Toulson dissenting) held that the parking charge was not out of proportion to the legitimate interest to be protected. Lords Neuberger and Sumption (with whom Lords Carnwath and Clarke agreed on this point) said at [99] that although ParkingEye was not liable to suffer a loss as a result of overstaying motorists, it had a legitimate interest in charging them which extended beyond the recovery of any loss. ParkingEye met its costs from the charges for breaches by the motorists. It was also relevant that the landowner had a legitimate interest in the scheme applied by ParkingEye, including the receipt of a fee from ParkingEye to run the scheme and also to ensure adequate parking for customers of the retailer tenants. The landowner's interest was relevant because the penal character of the scheme could not depend on facts which a motorist might not reasonably know such as whether the landowner operates it himself or employs a contractor like ParkingEye to operate it. **15–012I**

(1) *Nature of liquidated damages and penalties*

Insert a new note at the end of the paragraph: **15–013**

NOTE 50a: Recent authorities, however, indicate that, even if the stipulated sum is not a genuine pre-estimate of loss, it will not be regarded as a penalty if there is a commercial justification for it: see the *Makdessi* and *Edgeworth* cases as referred to at paras 15–012I and 15–012L, above.

Insert a new paragraph after para.15–021:

The circumstances in which the rules about contractual penalties are invoked were novel in *ParkingEye Ltd v Beavis* (see para.15–012D, above). The overstaying charge was intended to deter from breach and was in no way a genuine pre-estimate of loss, there being indeed no loss at all to the claimant company. Despite this, the Supreme Court sensibly held the overstaying charge to be enforceable. **15–021A**

(2) *Effect of holding a stipulated sum to be liquidated damages or a penalty*

15–022   Insert a new note at the end of the paragraph:

(a) Sum held to be liquidated damages NOTE 76A: However, as pointed out by Leggatt J in *MSC Mediterranean Shipping Co SA v Cottonex Anstalt* [2015] EWHC 283 (Comm), in assessing whether a stipulated sum is or is not a penalty, the mitigation principle must be taken into account in comparing with the stipulated sum what the claimant would have recovered in the absence of the stipulated sum: *ibid.* at [113].

15–023   NOTE 77: Add at the end of the note: The *Bath* case was applied in *AB v CD* [2014] EWCA Civ 229. At [30], Underhill LJ (with whom Ryder and Laws LJJ agreed) said that a claimant will still need to show that if the threatened breach occurs then there is a substantial risk of unrecoverable loss due to the liquidated damages provision. But once this is shown there will be a discretion to award an injunction. Ryder LJ would have gone further and seen this as one factor in a test for whether it is "just in all the circumstances" to confine a claimant to damages (at [32]).

3. RULES FOR DISTINGUISHING LIQUIDATED DAMAGES FROM PENALTIES

(2) *The circumstances must be viewed as at the time when the contract was made*

Insert a new paragraph after para.15–030:

15–030A   An unusual situation arose in *MSC Mediterranean Shipping Co SA v Cottonex Anstalt* [2016] EWCA Civ 789, discussed at paras 9–030A to 9–030C. A contract of carriage by sea provided that for 14 days after the discharge of the cargo in the containers the shipper was entitled to retain the containers without charge, after which time container demurrage was payable indefinitely at a specified daily rate. The Court of Appeal held that the question did not arise because the carrier was not entitled to affirm the contract so that he could obtain demurrage indefinitely. However, as Moore-Bick LJ nevertheless explained at [47], the provision was not penal simply because it fixed no express limit on the period of the charterer's liability. The liability was not unlimited because general principles of law, such as those restraining affirmation, imposes a limit on the scope of the charterer's liability.

4. MAIN TYPES OF CONTRACT IN WHICH THE RULES HAVE BEEN DEVELOPED

(2) *Types of contract where the stipulated sum is generally liquidated damages*

15–073   **(a) Charterparties: improper detention of ship by charterer.** Insert in the text after the second sentence of the paragraph: Stipulated sums payable to carriers of goods in their shipping containers, graduated to the length of time after they should have been returned to the carrier, have today come to be classified as demurrage, specifically as container demurrage. *MSC Mediterranean Shipping Co SA v Cottonex Anstalt* [2016] EWCA Civ 789, discussed at paras 9–030A to 9–030C and 15–030A above, is such a case, and probably the first such case.

CHAPTER 16

VINDICATORY DAMAGES

2. VINDICATORY DAMAGES FOR INFRINGEMENT OF A RIGHT

16–014 Insert a new note after "actionable *per se*" on the last line but four of the paragraph:

NOTE 50a: The Court of Appeal in *Bostridge v Oxleas NHS Foundation Trust* [2015] EWCA Civ 79 held that where, unlike the defendant Secretary of State for the Home Department in *Lumba*, the defendant NHS trust had no power lawfully to detain the claimant, a mentally disordered patient, but he could and would have been lawfully detained anyway by a third party, there was still an entitlement only to nominal damages as there was no loss. Delivering the only reasoned judgment in the Court of Appeal, Vos LJ recorded that the appellant's counsel had disavowed any argument based upon the Earl of Halsbury's famous dictum in *The Mediana* [1900] A.C. 113 at 117, discussed at para.35–044, below.

Insert new paragraphs after para.16–015:

16–016 Any doubt that remained has now been removed by the unanimous application of the decision in *Lumba* in *R (O) v Secretary of State for the Home Department (Bail for Immigration Detainees)* [2016] UKSC 19; [2016] 1 W.L.R. 1717. The Supreme Court held that although the Home Secretary had unlawfully failed to apply her policy to the claimant's detention, if the claim for judicial review were permitted to proceed the result would be a declaration that detention was unlawful and an award of only nominal damages. Since the decision of the Supreme Court provided sufficient vindication, the Court of Appeal had been correct to refuse permission for the claim to proceed.

16–017 The consequence of the decision in *Lumba* is that the law is left in an unsatisfactory state. In defamation cases awards are made which include an element to vindicate the right to reputation independently of any financial loss or subjective distress, pain or suffering. One possibility is that the vindication

[59]

awards in defamation cases might be re-rationalised as cases where compensation is awarded for likely future consequences if the libel "emerges from its lurking place at some future date": *Broome v Cassell & Co Ltd* [1972] A.C. 1027, 1071 (Lord Hailsham) cited with approval in *R (on the application of Lumba (Congo)) v Secretary of State for the Home Department* [2011] UKSC 12, [2012] 1 A.C. 245, 316 [223] (Lord Collins).

However, vindicatory damages appear to have re-emerged after *Lumba* in *Representative Claimants (Gulati) v MGN Ltd* [2015] EWCA Civ 1291. In that case, appeals were brought by MGN Ltd, the proprietor of the *Daily Mirror*, *The Sunday People* and *The Sunday Mirror* newspapers, against awards of damages to eight claimants for misuse of private information by "hacking" of their telephone messages. The damages included separate awards for hacking which did not lead to publication, hacking which led to publishing of articles, general distress, and aggravated damages. The awards ranged in total from £72,500 to £260,250. The highest single award for hacking (although combined in this instance with distress) was £85,000 for Mr Yentob, a BBC executive who made extensive use of his voicemail. His voicemail contained an enormous amount of entertainment-related material of interest to journalists. His phone was hacked at least twice a day for a period of about 7 years.

One ground of appeal was that the awards should have been limited to damages for distress. MGN submitted that by making an award of both damages for distress and damages for misuse of private information the primary judge's approach was contrary to the rejection of vindicatory damages by a majority of the Supreme Court in *R (Lumba) v Secretary of State for the Home Department* [2012] 1 A.C. 245. The primary judge had held that an award for the mere infringement of the claimants' rights should be made because if damages were limited to an award for distress, a person who suffered no distress or died before the discovery of the wrong would receive no compensation. Delivering the judgment with which the other members of the Court of Appeal agreed, Arden LJ said (at [46], [48]) that the damages were not to "vindicate" a right but were "to compensate for the loss or diminution of a right to control formerly private information and for the distress that the respondents could justifiably have felt because their private information had been exploited". This award of damages simply for the act of hacking is consistent with cases in which substantial damages have been awarded for photographing a child even though the child suffered no distress (*AAA v Associated Newspapers Ltd* [2012] EWHC 2103 QB, *Weller v Associated Newspapers Ltd* [2014] E.M.L.R. 24 (appeal dismissed on other grounds: [2015] EWCA Civ 1176)).

The award of damages for the loss of a right to control information looks a lot like an award of vindicatory damages. A loss of control, or loss of autonomy, occurs in almost every tortious or contractual wrong. By itself, "loss of autonomy" is not necessarily a loss in the sense of an adverse consequence. If I am about to step off the curb into the path of an oncoming car and you push me backwards then I will have lost autonomy as a result of your actions. But my loss of the autonomy to be run over by a car is not a loss in the sense of being factually worse off. It is necessary to identify the sense in which the loss of control that a person encounters over his or her life has adverse consequences as an undesired intrusion into the person's life. The concept of damages simply for the loss of a "right to control formerly private information" should not be understood as suggesting, literally, that the compensation is for the loss of a right. A right is a normative concept. A loss of a right is therefore only a normative loss. It is not a loss experienced in the real world. The position of the representative claimants is not affected in any way merely as a result of loss of any normative right. The real loss is a consequential loss such as distress suffered, or any other consequences experienced by the claimant as a result of the infringement. If there are no real consequences then there should be no damages for loss. In *Murray v Ministry of Defence* [1988] 1 W.L.R. 692, Lord Griffiths, with whom the remainder of the House of Lords agreed, said that only nominal damages would be awarded where a person is falsely imprisoned but suffered no loss and no distress because he was released before he found out that he had been falsely imprisoned.

If the award of damages for the claimant's "lost right to control private information" is to be justified independently of distress, it might only be justified as an award of damages which is restitutionary, representing the benefit that the defendant derived from the wrongdoing. This point is explained in Ch.14.

The decision in *Gulati* was carefully considered by Richard Spearman QC **16–018** sitting as a Deputy Judge in the Chancery Division in *Burrell v Clifford* [2016] EWHC 294 (Ch). The claim concerned a breach of confidence and misuse of private information given in confidence by Mr Burrell, the butler to the late Diana, Princess of Wales to Mr Clifford. Mr Burrell provided the confidential information to a publicist, Mr Clifford who, in turn, provided that information to News of the World. But it was never published by News of the World. The contents of the information provided by Mr Burrell were "relatively saccharine" ([155]). The Deputy Judge focused closely on the distress suffered by Mr Burrell which was described as being greater than that which would have been suffered by "an individual of more robust disposition" yet not too remote. The total compensation awarded was £5,000.

BOOK THREE

VARIOUS GENERAL FACTORS IN THE ASSESSMENT
OF DAMAGES

CHAPTER 18

THE AWARDING OF INTEREST

IV. CALCULATION OF THE AMOUNT OF INTEREST

1. PERIOD OF TIME FOR WHICH INTEREST IS AWARDED

(3) Application of the above principles to personal injury and wrongful death cases

18–090   In the first sentence, after the words "for personal injury claims and since *Cookson v Knowles*" add the following words ", as varied by the decision of the Supreme Court in *Knauer (Widower and Administrator of the Estate of Sally Ann Knauer) (Appellant) v Ministry of Justice (Respondent)* [2016] UKSC 9 in relation to calculation of the multiplier at the date of trial".

(4) Effect of delay on time to and from which interest runs

18–098   NOTE 389: Add at the end of the note: *Network Rail Infrastructure Ltd v Hardy* [2015] EWHC 1460 (TTC) is a case other than of personal injury where delay, which was pleaded, was held not to cut down the interest award. The earlier judgment on the damages to be awarded is at para.37–028, below.

2. RATE OF INTEREST AWARDED

(2) Cases in the Commercial Court and analogous cases

18–121   NOTE 553: Add at the end of the note: The claim for interest was in US dollars in *Somasteel SARL v Coresteel DMCC* Unreported 20 April 2015, an action for non-delivery of goods sold, but, since the buyer's interests were in Morocco and its financial interests arose in Morocco, interest was awarded at the historical Moroccan rate.

CHAPTER 19

THE EFFECT OF CHANGES IN VALUE

3. CHANGES IN THE VALUE OF MONEY

(1) *General change in the internal value of sterling over the years*

Add at the end of the paragraph: This 10 per cent uplift is not discretionary. **19–012** Claimants are entitled to it, unless they entered into a conditional fee arrangement: *Summers v Bundy* [2016] EWCA Civ 126.

BOOK FOUR

PARTICULAR CONTRACTS AND TORTS

CHAPTER 22

THE MEASURE OF DAMAGES IN CONTRACT AND TORT COMPARED

Remove the last four sentences of the paragraph, i.e. from the words "This **22–009** question has not yet been faced by the courts but one day, hopefully soon, it will have to be" to the end.

Insert the following new paragraphs after para.22–009:

The approach suggested in the previous paragraph would not entail depriving **22–009A** the victim of contractual and tortious negligence of the entitlement to take advantage of the longer limitation period available in the tort. The exclusion of the tort remedy on remoteness grounds is geared to what risks the contracting parties have undertaken, a consideration that has no application to the availability of limitation periods.

The approach suggested in the previous paragraph was approved in *Wellesley* **22–009B** *Partners LLP v Withers LLP* [2015] EWCA Civ 1146 [74] (Floyd LJ); [145]-[163] (Roth J); [183]-[187] (Longmore LJ), and applied with the effect that the test for recoverability of damage for economic loss was held to be the same whether the action was brought for a tort or for breach of contract. The test to be applied in cases of concurrent liability was the contractual one because the existence of concurrent liability should not upset the agreed consensus particularly given that the tortious duty arose out of the same assumption of responsibility as exists under the contract ([76], [80] (Floyd LJ); [186] (Longmore LJ)).

Two of the judges in *Wellesley Partners* suggested that the principle might **22–009C** even go further. At [163] and [187], Roth J and Longmore LJ said that the contractual test might apply even if there were no concurrent liability but if the tortious liability were based on the *Hedley Byrne* principle of liability based on an assumption of responsibility in a "relationship equivalent to contract". There is great merit in this suggestion. As Murphy JA and I explained in *Swick Nominees Pty Ltd v Leroi International Inc (No.2)* [2015] WASCA 35 [369]–[372], the *Hedley Byrne* doctrine reaffirmed a very old principle that would today be seen as contractual, not tortious.

Broadly, the case involved negligence by a firm of solicitors in drafting the **22–009D** changes to a partnership agreement for a headhunting firm to provide for a partnership share for an investment bank. The solicitors had been told by Mr Channing, a star operator for the headhunting firm, to include an option permitting the bank to reduce its share *after* 42 months. Instead, the solicitors included a clause permitting the reduction *within* 41 months. The investment bank reduced its share, and withdrew capital, within 12 months. The headhunters said that they lost profits including a loss because Mr Channing's time had been occupied with the dispute with the investment bank which caused them to lose a chance of obtaining lucrative business with an investment bank called Nomura. The trial judge awarded around £1 million for that head of damages for the lost chance of obtaining Nomura's business.

One ground of appeal was whether that loss was too remote. The Court of Appeal considered that there were differences between the remoteness test for breach of contract and the test for a tort. At [74], Floyd LJ explained that there were parallels between the test in cases of breach of contract and in cases of torts. In both there were two limbs. The first limb in contract ("reasonable contemplation") is comparable, although more restrictive, than it is for torts ("reasonable foreseeability" which could include highly unusual or unlikely damage). The second limb involving "assumption of responsibility" in contract and "scope of duty" for a tort, also involves similar, but not identical, enquiries. But where the liability was concurrent, and possibly also where the liability was *Hedley Byrne* liability based on an assumption of responsibility in a relationship akin to contract, the contractual approach should prevail.

BOOK FOUR

PART ONE

CONTRACT

SALE OF GOODS

I. BREACH BY SELLER

1. NON-DELIVERY

Insert a new note at the end of the paragraph: **23–003**

NOTE 4a: The loss of profits claim for breach by non-delivery under the first of two contracts for the sale of steel billets in *Somasteel SARL v Coresteel DMCC* Unreported 29 April 2015, got nowhere as there was held to be an available market. Therefore s.51(3) applied.

(1) *Normal measure*

NOTE 11: Add at the end of the note: Nominal damages were awarded for **23–004** breach by non-delivery under the second of two contracts for the sale of steel billets in *Somasteel SARL v Coresteel DMCC* Unreported 29 April 2015, as the market price had fallen well below the contract price.

23–014   NOTE 48: Add at the end of the note: Interestingly, in *Somasteel SARL v Coresteel DMCC* Unreported 29 April 2015, an action for non-delivery of goods sold where there was held to be an available market, the trial judge arrived at a market price not by concentrating on the buyer's actions, as the cases preceding above do, but by taking the average price based on similar contracts that the seller had made around the time of the contract.

(2) *Consequential losses*

23–023   Insert a new note at the end of the paragraph:

NOTE 105a: One item of recovery in the complex damages case of *Thai Airways International Public Co Ltd v KI Holdings Co Ltd* [2015] EWHC 1250 (Comm), where there was non-delivery of a number of economy class seats sold for installation in aircraft, was the additional cost of purchasing of replacement seats, subject to certain credits. See at *ibid.* at [20] with [141] et seq., and the case in detail at para.9–006A, above.

2. DELAYED DELIVERY

(2) *Consequential losses*

23–044   Insert a new note at the end of the paragraph:

NOTE 189a: One item of recovery in the complex damages case of *Thai Airways International Public Co Ltd v KI Holdings Co Ltd* [2015] EWHC 1250 (Comm), where there was delayed delivery of a number of economy class seats sold for installation in aircraft, was the additional cost of purchasing, before delivery had taken place, of replacement seats, subject to certain credits. See *ibid.* at [18], [19] with [141] et seq., and the case in detail at para.9–006A, above.

4. BREACH OF CONDITION OR WARRANTY AS TO QUALITY, FITNESS OR DESCRIPTION; GOODS ACCEPTED

23–060   Insert a new note at the end of the paragraph:

NOTE 254a: A buyer is entitled to recover for consequential losses arising from the breach of warranty on top of recovery for the normal measure. The arbitration award was therefore held to be wrong in *Saipol SA v Inerco Trade SA* [2014] EWHC 2211 (Comm) as it had limited the buyer of sunflower seed oil, contaminated in the shipping of it, to the normal measure by applying s.53(3) instead of s.53(2).

I. Breach by Seller

(1) *Normal measure*

Add at the end of the paragraph: However, in *OMV Petrom SA v Glencore*   **23–069**
International AG [2016] EWCA Civ 778, the Court of Appeal, without deciding,
seemed to indicate a preference for the view of the Court of Appeal in *Slater v
Hoyle & Smith* [1920] 2 K.B. 11 over that of the later Court of Appeal in *Bence
Graphics v Fasson* [1998] Q.B. 87. The Court of Appeal observed, at [45], that
the reliance by Auld LJ in *Bence* on the Privy Council decision in *Wertheim v
Chicoutimi Pulp Co* [1911] A.C. 301 was upon a decision which Scrutton LJ
thought was erroneous. But, as we have seen above at para.23–042 there is a
simple explanation to the concerns of Scrutton LJ about the decision in
Wertheim.

(2) *Consequential losses*

Insert a new note at the end of the paragraph: **23–086**

NOTE 373a: The Court of Appeal in *Stacey v Autosleeper Group Ltd* [2014]
EWCA Civ 1551 (facts in note to para.8–147, above) endorsed the trial judge's
allowing recovery of costs paid to the third party, but not in full as they had been
increased by the buyer's unreasonable conduct: *ibid.* at [24], [25].

CHAPTER 27

SALE OF SHARES AND LOAN OF STOCK

I. BREACH BY SELLER

2. OTHER BREACHES

Add at the end of the first sentence of the paragraph: This is confirmed and **27–008**
applied in all of three cases in the circumstances of which it was held that events
subsequent to the breach were not to be taken into account. These are *Ageas (UK)
Ltd v Kwik-Fit (GB) Ltd* [2014] EWHC 2178 QB, *Hut Group Ltd v Nobahar-
Cookson* [2014] EWHC 3842 QB and *Bir Holdings Ltd v Mehta* [2014] EWHC
3903 Ch, considered in detail at para.10–120, above.

CHAPTER 30

CONTRACTS OF CARRIAGE

II. BREACH BY CARGO OWNER

1. Failure to Supply Cargo

(2) *Consequential losses*

Insert a new paragraph after para.30–075:

In *Louis Dreyfus Commodities Suisse SA v MT Maritime Management BV,* **30–075A**
"MTM Hong Kong" [2015] EWHC 2505 (Comm) Males J considered whether
damages should be restricted to the losses suffered up until the point when the
contract voyage would have come to an end. The charterers submitted that *Smith
v McGuire* (1858) 3 H & N 554 permitted only the recovery of losses until the
point that the contract voyage had ended, although there was no claim in that case
for losses beyond the point when the contract voyage had ended. The difference
was substantial. The *Smith v McGuire* (1858) 3 H & N 554 measure would have
led to an award in favour of the shipowner of US $478,386. The amount which

was awarded by the arbitral tribunal resulted in an award of almost three times this amount.

The reason for the difference was that additional consequential loss was suffered by the owners because performance of the contract voyage would not only have enabled the owners to earn the freight payable under the voyage charter but it would also have ensured that the vessel was situated in Europe without delay at the conclusion of the voyage, ready to take advantage of the higher freights available in the North Atlantic market. The charterers' repudiation meant that the owners had to mitigate by taking a different charter, which delayed the repositioning of the vessel causing the loss of two lucrative transatlantic charters that could have been performed in the same time as the mitigation charter. The primary judge upheld the arbitral tribunal's award of these consequential losses.

CHAPTER 31

CONTRACTS OF EMPLOYMENT

I. BREACH BY EMPLOYER

2. Wrongful Dismissal

(1) *Normal measure*

NOTE 54: Add at the end of the note: *Lavarack* and *Horkulak* come under discussion in *IBM United Kingdom Holdings Ltd v Dalgleish* [2015] EWHC 389 Ch where there was not wrongful dismissal but breach of the duty of trust and confidence. See the case at para.31–031 n.185a, below.   **31–011**

3. Breach of Obligation of Trust and Confidence

Insert a new note at the end of the paragraph: **31–031**

NOTE 185a: Breach of the obligation of trust and confidence again features in *IBM United Kingdom Holdings Ltd v Dalgleish* [2015] EWHC 389 Ch, which involved an employer's scheme to vary the contractual rights of employees by making their salaries non-pensionable in return for salary increases. Warren J's judgment is concerned with the entitlement to damages rather than with their assessment but there is much discussion on damages (*ibid.* at [139]–[178]). See the references to the case at paras.10–111 n.494 and 31–011 n.54, above.

II. BREACH BY EMPLOYEE

3. MISCELLANEOUS BREACHES

31–040   Add at the end of the paragraph: In *Merlin Financial Consultants v Cooper* [2015] EWHC 1196 QB, where the employee was in breach of a restrictive covenant by setting up a competing business on the termination of his employment, the employer was awarded damages based on the profits that it would have made from the clients who had left, subject to a deduction, as an expense, of the amount payable to a replacement employee, and subject in addition to a percentage deduction from these profits as the trial judge was of the view that some of the clients would have left anyway, even if the employee had not been in breach of his contractual obligations: see *ibid.* at [74]–[83].

CHAPTER 32

CONTRACTS FOR PROFESSIONAL AND OTHER SERVICES

II. BREACH BY THE PARTY RENDERING THE SERVICES

(A) *IN GENERAL*

Insert a new paragraph after para.32–003:

The basic principles concerning breach by a party rendering services ought to **32–003A** be the same as the principles concerning breach by a party providing goods. The similarity is most apparent where the services involve the provision of work which needs to be obtained elsewhere due to non-performance.

In *Gartell & Son (a firm) v Yeovil Town Football & Athletic Club Ltd* [2016] EWCA Civ 62, Gartell & Son carried out work for Yeovil Football and Athletic Club Ltd on their athletic pitches. Yeovil refused to pay saying that the work was defective and counterclaimed for the cost of works rendered necessary by the breach of contract. The Court of Appeal upheld the conclusion of the primary judge that the work performed had been so defective that there had been no improvement to the pitch. This meant that Yeovil was discharged from its obligation to pay the contract price. However, the primary judge had awarded Yeovil the entire costs of the performance of the work by another party. The Court of Appeal held that this was an error. The damages are to be assessed by reference to "the *additional* cost to Yeovil of arranging for the work contracted for to be done by someone else, but Gartell cannot be denied payment and then rendered liable for the entire cost of obtaining a substitute performance". The Court of Appeal explained that the situation is analogous to the case of non-delivery of goods. There, the purchaser's damages are "the additional amount he reasonably has to pay for the goods from another supplier. The purchaser does not get the substitute goods for nothing" ([33]).

(B) *PARTICULAR CATEGORIES*

1. SOLICITORS

(1) *Pecuniary loss*

Insert a new paragraph after para.32–009:

32–009A   Finally, as with all loss, negligent advice by solicitors can lead to a reduction in liability if the client fails to mitigate the loss. This occurred in *LSREF III Wight Ltd v Gateley LLP* [2016] EWCA Civ 359 where a firm of solicitors negligently omitted from their advice to a lender any reference to the effect of an insolvency forfeiture clause in a lease over a property provided as security. The loss of value was £240,000. But the lessor offered to remove the clause for £150,000. The lender unreasonably refused and therefore failed to mitigate its loss.

Insert a new paragraph after para.32–012:

32–012A   These principles concerning recovery of the normal loss are, of course, subject to the usual rules including mitigation and remoteness. Hence, in *Bacciottini & anor v Gotelee and Goldsmith (A Firm)* [2016] EWCA Civ 170 the normal measure of loss suffered was not recovered when solicitors failed to advise the appellant purchasers of a planning restriction on property they purchased for development. The reason that the normal recovery was denied was because the purchasers mitigated their loss by successfully removing the planning restriction.

II. Breach by the Party rendering the services

2. Surveyors and Valuers

(1) *Purchasers of property negligently surveyed or valued*

Insert a new paragraph after para.32–050:

Although these cases concern the normal measure of damages, that normal **32–050A** measure is not immutable. In *Bacciottini & anor v Gotelee and Goldsmith (A Firm)* [2016] EWCA Civ 170, Davis LJ (Lloyd Jones and Underhill LJJ agreeing) explained that the normal loss at the date of breach suffered by the appellants might have been the difference between the price they paid and the value of the property without the planning restriction but the appellants had successfully had the planning restriction removed. Therefore the normal loss could not be recovered. The Court of Appeal observed that the question really is whether, in all the circumstances of the case, the normal measure properly reflects the overriding compensatory rule (at [48] referring to *Pankhania v London Borough of Hackney* [2004] EWHC 323 (Ch) [21]).

BOOK FOUR

PART TWO

TORT

TORTS AFFECTING GOODS: DAMAGE AND DESTRUCTION

I. DAMAGE

(B) *CONSEQUENTIAL LOSSES*

1. EXPENSES OTHER THAN THE COST OF REPAIR

(1) *Expenses made necessary*

Insert a new paragraph after para.35–024:

There being a whole range of basic hire rates offered on the market for **35–024A** vehicles generally and therefore for vehicles of the type that it was reasonable for the particular claimant to hire, judges at the lower level have had much difficulty in deciding on the basic hire rate appropriate in the case before them. The Court of Appeal in *Stevens v Equity Syndicate Management Ltd* [2015] EWCA Civ 93 has now given guidance. The claimant there had entered into a credit hire agreement but, being held not to be impecunious, was entitled to claim only the basic hire rate. Accordingly, the Court of Appeal started by considering how the basic hire element in the total charged under the credit hire agreement was to be ascertained. It proving impractical to find this out as it would require disclosure and analysis at a cost in excess of the value of the claim, the court resorted to looking at basic hire rates available in the claimant's locality, which is what the lower courts in the case had attempted to do: *ibid.* at [30]–[32]. If, as is likely, there is a range of rates, the court must seek out the lowest reasonable rate quoted by a mainstream supplier, or in the absence of a mainstream supplier by a local reputable supplier, for a vehicle of the kind in issue to a reasonable person in the position of the claimant: *ibid.* at [32]–[40]. Kitchin LJ's judgment, the only reasoned one given, reviews the major authorities and merits study.

35–025   Add at the end of the paragraph: The Court of Appeal has now made it crystal clear in *Zurich Insurance Plc v Sameer* [2014] EWCA Civ 357 that a claimant's entitlement to rely on impecuniosity goes to the duration of hire as much as to the rate of hire. Impecuniosity could justify a higher level of award where the claimant continued to hire due to inability to pay for repairs or to buy a replacement car: *ibid.* at [9(4)]. The case itself was concerned only with the interpretation of an order debarring the claimant, whose car was a write-off, from relying on his impecuniosity and with whether the order covered the duration of hiring as well as the rate of hire. A further issue mentioned but not argued was whether the rules of mitigation required the claimant to claim on his insurance policy and with the proceeds buy a replacement car. The court said that, while this was an interesting question of some importance, it was for another day: *ibid.* at [41]–[43].

4. LOSS OF USE OF CHATTELS WHICH ARE NOT PROFIT-EARNING

(2) *Amount of such damages*

35–059   The words "based on te capital" should be "based on the capital".

NOTE 305: Add at the end of the note: See also *Bee v Jenson* [2007] EWCA Civ 923.

CHAPTER 37

TORTS AFFECTING LAND

I. DAMAGE

3. CONSEQUENTIAL LOSSES

(1) *Loss of profits and expenses incurred*

Add at the end of the paragraph: **37–028**

In *Network Rail Infrastructure Ltd v Handy* [2015] EWHC 1175 (TTC), Akenhead J described the proceedings as involving a sense of "déjà vu". Again, when the defendants damaged the railway track in this case several different points were raised that had not been previously raised, or had been conceded. Again, the defendants were found to be liable to pay damages for the losses suffered by Network Rail under the agreed formula.

One argument made by the defendants was that the imposition of damages based on a formula that was agreed between the claimant and third parties could be unreasonable. Akenhead J, following comments in the Court of Appeal in the *Conarken Group* case, explained that there is no overarching or separate principle that requires damages to be reasonable as between claimant and defendant. However, if the amount of agreed damages were extremely large, then even if those damages had been suffered they might be reduced based on principles of causation, remoteness, mitigation, or a focus on the scope of the tortious duty.

Another issue was whether economic loss was recoverable in a trespass action when there was no physical damage to land. It was held that neither in negligence nor in trespass was physical damage necessary. In negligence cases it is sufficient if the breach of duty results in substances or physical things being deposited on the property in question in more than a de minimis manner such that the property cannot be used or enjoyed as it otherwise would or could be if the substances or physical things had not been so deposited. In trespass cases, economic losses can be recovered even if there is no damage to, or fouling of, the land. An example given was a defendant who trespasses by parking a fleet of lorries on the claimant's land. Even if there is no physical damage to the land a reasonable charge could be recovered based on the income the claimant land-owner might reasonably have charged for lorries to park there. This would be equivalent to a loss of income.

CHAPTER 38

TORTS CAUSING PERSONAL INJURY

[95]

Insert a new paragraph after para.38–002:

38–002A   A preliminary question of fact in every personal injury case is whether
actionable damage has been suffered. In instances such as pleural plaques, no
actionable damage was found to have occurred: *Rothwell v Chemical and
Insulating Company Ltd* [2007] UKHL 39, [2008] 1 A.C. 281. In that case, at [7],
Lord Hoffmann explained that actionable damage is "an abstract concept of
being worse off, physically or economically". This could not be proved by
sensitisation from exposure at work to platinum salts in *Greenway v Johnson
Matthey Plc* [2014] EWHC 3957, QB (see *ibid.* para.13 et seq. and the facts at
para.8–134, above) any more than with the pleural plaques in *Rothwell v Chemical and Insulating Co* [2008] A.C. 281 (at para.5–012 of the main work). See
also the decision of the same judge (Jay J) in *Saunderson v Sonae Industria (UK)
Ltd* [2015] EWHC 2264 QB [178]. However, the decision in *Carder v The
University of Exeter* [2016] EWCA Civ 790 emphasises that the conclusion
reached will be highly dependent upon particular facts. In that case, the Court of
Appeal considered whether the negligent exposure of Mr Carder by the appellant
to 2.3 per cent of the total lifetime dose of asbestos was "actionable damage".
The appellant submitted that the exposure had made and would make no difference to his symptoms, disability or prognosis. The Master of the Rolls (with
whom Gross and Christopher Clarke LJJ agreed) held that on the facts there had
been actionable damage because the severity of the disease had been increased to
a small, albeit not measurable, extent.

I. FORMS OF AWARD AND OF COMPENSATION

1. INTERIM AWARDS

38–005   NOTE 16: Add at the end of the note: Where with liability admitted the court
is satisfied that substantial damages will be awarded but it is currently difficult
to conclude accurately what sum will be recovered, the assessment must be
carried out on a conservative basis and the risk of overpayment avoided: *AS v
West Suffolk Hospital Trust* Unreported (as yet) 1 May 2015.

II. CERTAINTY OF LOSS

1. Changes before the Decision of the Court of First Instance

Insert a new note at the end of the paragraph: **38–040**

NOTE 128a: For a different approach to consecutive injuries, see *Reaney v University Hospital of North Staffordshire NHS Trust* [2014] EWHC 3016 QB at para.8–090 n.448, above.

IV. LOSS OF EARNING CAPACITY AND RELATED BENEFITS

(B) *CALCULATION OF THE MULTIPLICAND AND OF THE MULITPLER*

3. Adjustments for Variation in Annual Earnings Loss

(2) *Handicap in the labour market: then and now*

Insert a new paragraph after para.38–099:

The discussion in the immediately preceding paragraph supporting the survival **38–099A** of *Smith v Manchester* is also supported by the Explanatory Notes made by the Ogden Working Party that there will be circumstances in which the *Smith v Manchester* approach would still be appropriate. One of those circumstances arose in *Billett v Ministry of Defence* [2015] EWCA Civ 773. There, the claimant had suffered an injury to his feet whilst serving in the army. The trial judge had made an award of £99,062.04 based upon the Ogden Tables for loss of earning capacity. The Court of Appeal held that the Ogden Tables should not have been applied because there was no evidence of how the claimant would be classified within a scale of degree of impairment and if the Ogden Tables were applied without adjustment the award for future loss of earning capacity would be hopelessly unrealistic for the claimant who was pursuing his chosen career as a lorry driver without hindrance. The exercise of making an adjustment to the reduction factors in the Ogden Tables would be no more scientific than the broad brush judgment that the court makes when taking the *Smith v Manchester* approach. It was preferable to apply *Smith v Manchester* because: (i) the claimant was at the very margins of the definition of disability; (ii) his disability affected his activities outside work much more than it affected his work; and (iii) there was no rational basis for determining how the reduction factor should be adjusted. Applying *Smith v Manchester*, the Court of Appeal awarded an amount of £45,000 for the future earning capacity in place of the trial judge's award of £99,062.04.

5. ADJUSTMENTS WHERE LIFE EXPECTANCY IS CUT DOWN BY THE INJURY

(2) *The question of the lost years*

38–112   Insert a new note at the end of the paragraph:

NOTE 508a: In *Totham v King's College Hospital NHS Foundation Trust* [2015] EWHC 97 QB the trial judge also wished to see the *Croke* decision overruled as she agreed with the Court of Appeal's criticisms of it in *Iqbal*, which criticisms, as stated in this work, are thought to be misconceived.

7. ADJUSTMENTS TO THE MULTIPLIER FOR CONTINGENCIES

(2) *Contingencies other than mortality*

38–137   Add at the end of the paragraph: In some cases the Ogden criteria might not be applied at all. These cases will be where the degree of disability is very small, the effect upon a claimant's work is not significant, and there is no rational basis for determining how the reduction factor should be adjusted: *Billett v Ministry of Defence* [2015] EWCA Civ 773, discussed above at para.38–099A.

V. MEDICAL AND RELATED EXPENSES

(A) *EXPENSES INCLUDED*

1. MEDICAL EXPENSES

(1) *In general*

38–181   NOTE 798: Replace note with the following: In *Reaney v University Hospital of North Staffordshire NHS Trust* [2015] EWCA Civ 1119, the Court of Appeal, at paras 30-33, rejected the approach of Edwards-Stuart J in *Sklair v Haycock* [2009] EWHC 3328 QB. The Court of Appeal held that the causation question to be asked was whether the care required as a result of the accident was qualitatively different from that which would have been required but for the accident. This was different from a question, relevant to quantification of damages not causation, of "giving credit" for the costs that would have been avoided.

(2) *Medical treatment and care provided privately and provided by the National Health Service or by local authorities*

Insert a new paragraph after para.38–186:

V. Medical and Related Expenses

The passage into law of the Care Act 2014 has not altered these principles, although s.22 of that Act provides that the duties and powers to meet a person's needs for care and support are now qualified because, with limited exceptions, a local authority may not meet those needs by providing or arranging for the provision of a service or facility that is required to be provided under the National Health Service Act.   **38–186A**

2. Related Expenses

(4) *Living expenses*

Add at the end of the paragraph: In *Ellison v University Hospitals of Morecambe Bay NHS Foundation Trust* [2015] EWHC 366 QB the very substantial cost of installing and maintaining an in-home hydrotherapy pool was held justified as an item in the damages awarded since use of the pool was the one way of relieving the excessive pain suffered by the severely disabled child claimant: see the lengthy passage in the judgment at *ibid.* at [78]–[120].   **38–196**

(5) *Special accommodation expenses*

NOTE 902: Add at the end of the note: In *Ellison v University Hospitals of Morecambe Bay NHS Foundation Trust* [2015] EWHC 366 QB Warby J relied on Swift J's reasoning and judgment so as to hold, as with her, that there should be no deduction on account of any benefit to the child's parents from living free in the house suitable for the disabled child which was to be acquired; it was the child's claim and any such deduction would bring down the damages so as to leave the child under-compensated: see the passage in his judgment, which analyses other cases dealing with the issue, *ibid.* at [134]–[152].   **38–198**

(B) *GENERAL METHOD OF ASSESSMENT*

Add at the end of the paragraph: In *Manna (A Child) v Central Manchester University Hospitals NHS Foundation Trust* [2015] EWHC 2279 QB, Cox J applied Table 28, recognising (at [185]) that the application of Table 1 would cause a double discount.   **38–216**

(C) *THE DEDUCTIBILITY OF COLLATERAL BENEFITS*

4. Care provided Gratuitously by Relatives and others

(2) *Amount to be awarded*

NOTE 1066: Add at the end of the note: *Evans* was applied in *FM v Ipswich Hospital NHS Trust* [2015] EWHC 775 QB, giving a discount of 25 per cent in preference to the defendant's proposal of a one third discount.   **38–230**

38–231   Insert a new note at the end of the paragraph:

NOTE 1079a: Where in *Totham v King's College Hospital NHS Foundation Trust* [2015] EWHC 97 QB a mother had given up a well-paid job to care for her daughter who was brain damaged at birth, the trial judge's award of only the commercial rate discounted in the usual way is surely wrong: see *ibid.* at [23]–[28].

VI. NON-PECUNIARY DAMAGE

4. LEVEL OF AWARDS

38–276   Add at the end of the paragraph: Courts do not have discretion in awarding the *Simmons v Castle* 10 per cent uplift, even if the uplift would give the claimant a windfall: *Summers v Bundy* [2016] EWCA Civ 126. The rationale behind this is that considerations of clarity and consistency override those of perfect justice in every case. The alternative, of a discretionary approach, would lead to complete uncertainty and inconsistency throughout England and Wales and difficulties in calculating and determining the form and amount of Part 36 offers or without prejudice proposals of settlement: *Summers v Bundy* [2016] EWCA Civ 126 at [21]–[22].

CHAPTER 39

TORTS CAUSING DEATH

[101]

I. CLAIMS FOR THE BENEFIT OF THE DECEASED'S DEPENDANTS

(B) *THE STATUTORY MEASURE OF DAMAGES*

2. THE VALUE OF THE DEPENDENCY

39–029   NOTE 159: Add at the end of the note: See for a high percentage chance, at 80 per cent, *Hayes v South East Coast Ambulance Service NHS Foundation Trust* [2015] EWHC 18 QB (divorced couple had come together again even with talk of remarriage: *ibid.* at [146]–[149]).

(3) *Calculation of the multiplicand and of the multiplier*

39–056   Delete the whole paragraph and replace with: The illogical reasoning of the courts in *Cookson v Knowles* and *Graham v Dodds* led to lower courts trying to distinguish the cases on inventive grounds, and openly critiquing the two decisions. One such example is Nelson J in *White v ESAB Group (UK) Ltd* [2002] P.I.Q.R. Q6, p.76 who felt himself bound by the earlier House of Lords decisions to calculate the multiplier from the date of death, although he personally was persuaded of the merits and correctness of the new thinking (at [27] and [43]). The Court of Appeal twice endorsed Nelson J, stating that it found his reasoning cogent: *H v S* [2003] W.B. 965 CA; *A. Train & Sons Ltd v Fletcher* [2008] EWCA Civ 413 CA.

Cookson v Knowles and *Graham v Dodds* finally came under close scrutiny in *Knauer (Widower and Administrator of the Estate of Sally Ann Knauer) (Appellant) v Ministry of Justice (Respondent)* [2016] UKSC 9. Ms Knauer died from mesothelioma as a result of the respondent's admitted negligence. The appeal to the Supreme Court concerned the assessment of damages owed to Ms Knauer's dependant widower. There was no dispute about the multiplicand in the Supreme Court. The question was whether the Supreme Court should apply the multiplier to that annual amount from the date of death (as required by *Cookson v Knowles* and *Graham v Dodds*) or at the date of trial. The Supreme Court, in a joint judgment delivered by Lord Neuberger and Lady Hale, refused to follow *Cookson v Knowles* and *Graham v Dodds*. The Supreme Court held that the reasoning was flawed, illogical and resulted in unfair outcomes. The Supreme Court held that the decisions were decided in a different era, when the calculation of damages was not as sophisticated. The Supreme Court held that the approach in *Cookson v Knowles* and *Graham v Dodds*—calculating the multiplier from the date of death—subrogated the key aim of an award of damages; to place the person who has been harmed by the wrongful acts of another in the position in which he or she would have been had the harm not been done. As explained above at para.39–054, the problem with the calculation of the multiplier from the date of death is that the multiplier includes a discount for early receipt of the money but for the period from death until trial the money has not been received.

Knauer has now definitively displaced the findings in *Cookson v Knowles* and *Graham v Dodds*, and upheld the more rational and fair approach of calculating the multiplier from the date of trial. For pre-trial losses the only difference from non-fatal cases will be that there will be a small deduction to take account of the possibility that before trial the deceased might have died or given up work in any event.

The Supreme Court in *Knauer* has therefore achieved the same result as the legislature in Scotland where s.7(1)(d) of the Damages (Scotland) Act 2011 provides that:

"any multiplier applied by the court—
    (i) is to run from the date of the interlocutor [i.e. judgment] awarding damages, and
    (ii) is to apply only in respect of future loss of support".

Delete the sentences from "This is still thought to be correct" until the **39–057** conclusion of that paragraph and replace with: This approach was adopted in the Supreme Court in *Knauer (Widower and Administrator of the Estate of Sally Ann Knauer) (Appellant) v Ministry of Justice (Respondent)* [2016] UKSC 9 where the Supreme Court definitively rejected *Cookson v Knowles* and *Graham v Dodds* and, following the approach in the Ogden Tables, held that the appropriate calculation is from the date of trial.

Replace the final sentence beginning with "And the position . . . " with the **39–061** following: And the decision of the Supreme Court in *Knauer (Widower and Administrator of the Estate of Sally Ann Knauer) (Appellant) v Ministry of Justice (Respondent)* [2016] UKSC 9, which held that the multiplier should be calculated from the date of trial in the case of a widower, must now put this date of assessment beyond doubt.

Replace the whole paragraph with the following: The decision in *Knauer* will **39–062** now remove the need for courts to attempt to reconcile the tension between calculation of the multiplier at the date of death (as was thought to be required for child dependents before *Knauer*) and the principle that damages should be calculated on the basis of known facts. That tension was most evident in *Corbett v Barking Havering and Brentwood Health Authority* [1991] 2 Q.B. 408 CA. The claim was on behalf of a child whose mother had died during his birth, and the trial judge took a multiplier of 12 based effectively not on the mother's life expectancy but on the shorter period of the child's dependency. Yet the child was already 11-and-a-half years old by the time the case came to trial, leaving the absurd position of having only a multiplier of 0.5 to cover the six or more years of dependency that were still in the future. The Court of Appeal was not prepared to depart from the assessment as at the date of death but held that the judge was entitled to take into account the facts as they were known at the date of the trial and to adjust the multiplier in the light of those facts. Purchas LJ said that he could "see no justification for denying the court the power" to do this: *Corbett v Barking Havering and Brentwood Health Authority* [1991] 2 Q.B. 408 CA [at 427A]; the multiplier was increased to 15. While respectfully agreeing with this result, except to comment that the multiplier should have been increased by more than three, there is thought to be much cogency in what was said by the dissenting Ralph Gibson LJ who reached, "after much hesitation", the contrary conclusion that there should be no adjustment to the multiplier of 12; the course taken by the majority, he said, "seems to me, in effect, to calculate the multiplier as at the date of trial": *Corbett v Barking Havering and Brentwood Health Authority* [1991] 2 Q.B. 408 CA [at 440H].

(4) *Particular Relationships*

39–083   NOTE 403: Insert at the beginning of the note: Cost of carers and a variety of other costs not agreed by the parties to the action were awarded in *Zambarda v Shipbreaking (Queensborough) Ltd* [2013] EWHC 2263 QB.

II. CLAIMS SURVIVING THE DEATH FOR THE BENEFIT OF THE DECEASED'S ESTATE

2. ACCRUED LOSSES OF THE DECEASED

(1) *Pecuniary losses*

39–125   Insert a new note before "Exceptionally" on line four of the paragraph:

NOTE 630a: A variety of costs were awarded in the estate action in *Zambarda v Shipbreaking (Queensborough) Ltd* [2013] EWHC 2263 QB.

(2) *Non-pecuniary losses*

39–126   Insert in the text after the indented citation from Parker LJ in the middle of the paragraph: For rather different reasons, the Court of Appeal in *Kadir v Mistry* [2014] EWCA Civ 1177 agreed with the trial judge's refusal to award any damages for pain and suffering. Diagnosis of cancer in the deceased had been negligently delayed. Had there been no delay the deceased would have suffered the same symptoms, although somewhat later and in the interim would have been subjected to painful treatment to deal with the cancer. Laws LJ, giving the only reasoned judgment, stressed that there were no special rules for assessing pain and suffering in estate claims; the criterion is, as always, to put the now deceased in the same position as he or she would have been if the negligence had not occurred: *ibid.* at [11], [12].

Add at the end of the paragraph: We have seen (at para.38–259, above) that, **39–127** while awards of damages for loss of expectation of life have been abolished, damages for pain and suffering may take into account suffering caused by awareness that expectation of life has been reduced. The Court of Appeal in *Kadir v Mistry* [2014] EWCA Civ 1177 (facts at para.39–126, above) differed from the trial judge and awarded damages for mental suffering on account of the deceased's belief that, had her cancer been diagnosed earlier, she would have had a chance of survival. The case is perhaps particular in that there was an award for mental distress at the contemplation of a reduced life span with no award for pain and suffering independently of this element.

ASSAULT AND FALSE IMPRISONMENT

I. ASSAULT

2. AGGRAVATION AND MITIGATION

Insert a new paragraph after para.40–007:

40–007A The same approach which recognises a substantial award of aggravated damages can be seen in *Mohidin v Commissioner of Police of the Metropolis* [2015] EWHC 2740 QB. In that case, one of the claimants was held to have been falsely imprisoned and assaulted by the police. His award for false imprisonment was £4,500 and, for the minor assault, £250. However, to these basic awards was added aggravated damages of £7,200 for the racially abusive and intimidating way in which the assault and false imprisonment was committed. However, in *KCR v The Scout Association* [2016] EWHC 587 QB, the decision in *Richardson v Howie* was relied upon. The claimant had been repeatedly sexually assaulted by his Cub Scout Group Leader but no aggravated damages were awarded. However, Judge McKenna sitting as a High Court judge, following *Richardson v Howie* as he was required to do and approaching the assessment of damages with that decision "very much in mind" ([29]), nevertheless appeared to recognise aggravated damages, sub silento, as part of the general damages award. His Honour made a general damages award of £48,000 and said that there would be no "separate" award of aggravated damages ([92]).

II. FALSE IMPRISONMENT

1. HEADS OF DAMAGE

40–014   NOTE 74: Insert at the beginning of the note: In *AXD v Home Office* [2016] EWHC 1617 QB, Jay J emphasised that *Thomson* was only a guideline and that it was decided more than a decade ago.

Add the following before the final sentence which begins "Yet far larger amounts were": Even greater than the base award of £12,500 in that case was the award in *Tarakhil v Home Office* [2015] EWHC 2845 QB, where Mr Tarakhil was unlawfully detained by the government in immigration detention for three weeks. His Honour Judge Thornton QC awarded £14,250 for the detention. It appears that in making this award the judge was influenced by the fact that the claimant was aware of the unlawful nature of the imprisonment and that it had a profound effect on him. Nevertheless, the judge also awarded £3,000 for psychiatric injury and £2,000 for aggravated damages. There appears to be some element of double counting here. A 10 per cent uplift was also then made, apparently applying *Simmons v Castle* [2012] EWCA Civ 1288; [2013] 1 W.L.R. 1239. But the comparative cases upon which the award had been based would also have incorporated this uplift so it appears that some double counting occurred.

40–015   Add at the end of the paragraph: On the other hand, in *Patel v Secretary of State for the Home Department* [2014] EWHC 501 (Admin) the seriousness of the misconduct of immigration officers, where the false imprisonment was for the comparatively short period of six days, was held to justify an award of £20,000, even before aggravated damages and exemplary damages (for which, see paras 40–023 and 40–025, below) were brought in. The case was considered under the Human Rights Act as well as under the common law of false imprisonment, the breaches of Human Rights Act articles adding significantly to the damages award: see *ibid.* at [330], [336]–[342]. As for the unlawful detention for 61 days of an unaccompanied asylum-seeking young person, this led in *AS v Secretary of State for the Home Department* [2015] EWHC 1331 QB to an award of £23,000, before aggravated damages were brought in (for which, see para.40–023, below). Again, the possibility of a modest award was brushed aside in *AXD v Home Office* [2016] EWHC 1617 QB, although the differences between the applicant and respondent illustrate the great uncertainty that still exists in this range of damages. The claimant's false imprisonment was for 20 months and 5 days and an award of £120,000 was sought by AXD. But £50,000–£55,000 was suggested by the Home Office. The primary judge, Jay J, awarded £80,000, noting the irrelevance of the allegation that his claim for refugee status should have been recognised sooner and his diagnosis of paranoid schizophrenia (because he was still fit to be detained and a mental health team is readily accessible). His award was modestly increased by fear of being returned to Somalia, and increased because he was kept in his cell for 21 hours a day and he experienced personal difficulties on account of his sexual orientation.

In the list of cases, after the reference to *R (on the application of Lumba* **40–018** *(Congo)) v Secretary of State for the Home Department*, add: *R (O) v Secretary of State for the Home Department (Bail for Immigration Detainees)* [2016] UKSC 19; [2016] 1 W.L.R. 1717.

NOTE 95: Add at the end of the note: A further such case is *The Queen (on the application of Mohammed) v The Secretary of State for the Home Department* [2014] EWHC 1898 (Admin). A different type of case in which only nominal damages were awarded for a false imprisonment is *Bostridge v Oxleas NHS Foundation Trust* [2015] EWCA Civ 79 where a mentally disordered patient had been unlawfully detained by an NHS trust.

Add at the end of the paragraph: There was an additional award for psychiatric **40–019** illness in *AS v Secretary of State for the Home Department* [2015] EWHC 1331 QB (facts at para.40–015, above).

3. Aggravation and Mitigation

Add at the end of the paragraph: Aggravated damages of £5,000 were awarded **40–023** in *AS v Secretary of State for the Home Department* [2015] EWHC 1331 QB where an unaccompanied asylum-seeking young person was unlawfully detained for 61 days. The aggravating features recognised by the trial judge are detailed at *ibid.* at [13]. Aggravated damages of £30,000 were awarded in *Patel v Secretary of State for the Home Department* [2014] EWHC 501 (Admin), with the aggravating factors summarised at *ibid.* at [332]; see the case at para.40–015, above. And aggravated damages of £2,300 (claimant 1) and £7,200 (claimant 2) were awarded in *Mohidin v Commissioner of Police of the Metropolis* [2015] EWHC 2740 QB, where false imprisonment and assault by police officers was accompanied by racial abuse and humiliation. Other than the most exceptional case, the outer limits of aggravated damages seem to be around the £30,000 mark. This is evidenced by the extraordinary conduct in *AXD v Home Office* [2016] EWHC 1617 QB where aggravated damages of £25,000 were awarded and the absence of bad faith meant that the case fell short of the line for an award of exemplary damages. The factors justifying aggravated damages included (i) senior officials refraining from taking responsibility for the serious delays that were accumulating with the knowledge that the claimant was suffering from paranoid schizophrenia, (ii) sub-optimal treatment for his schizophrenia for nearly a year, (iii) release of the claimant into the community without a proper welfare plan in place which led to his inevitable institutionalisation, abuse of alcohol, and homelessness, and (iv) failure to provide the claimant with unpublished information relating to returns to Mogadishu.

40–024   NOTE 134: Add at the end of the note: Separate awards continue to be made, as in *AS v Secretary of State for the Home Department* [2015] EWHC 1331 QB and in *Patel v Secretary of State for the Home Department* [2014] EWHC 501 (Admin): see paras 40–015 and 40–023, above.

4. EXEMPLARY DAMAGES

40–025   Add at the end of the paragraph: Exemplary damages, in the amount of £15,000, have now been awarded for arbitrary and oppressive conduct of immigration officers in *Patel v Secretary of State for the Home Department* [2014] EWHC 501 (Admin); see *ibid.* at [343] and the case at para.40–015, above.

CHAPTER 41

STATUTORY TORTS: DISCRIMINATION AND HARASSMENT

I. DISCRIMINATION

1. HEADS OF DAMAGE

(1) *Non-pecuniary loss*

NOTE 16: Add at the end of the note: Cases of discrimination heard in the **41–006**
Employment Tribunal do not attract the 10 per cent uplift in damages for non-
pecuniary loss introduced by *Simmons v Castle* [2013] 1 W.L.R. 1239 CA. It was
so held in *De Souza v Vinci Construction UK Ltd* March 2015 EAT, the reasons
for bringing in this uplift (for which see para.51–044, below) having no application to the Employment Tribunal. See too para.5–003 n.4, above.

Add at the end of the paragraph: There has been an appeal, [2014] EWCA Civ **41–007**
91, and, as predicted, the Court of Appeal endorsed the reduction, commenting
that there was no justification for a one-off offensive comment being placed in
the middle band: *ibid.* at [59].

2. AGGRAVATED DAMAGES

Insert a new paragraph after para.41–014:

The concerns of Underhill J are, however, highlighted by situations in which **41–014A**
the award of aggravated damages is made for injury to feelings caused by

discrimination and harassment where the basic award is made for a different tort such as assault or false imprisonment. In *Mohidin v Commissioner of Police of the Metropolis* [2015] EWHC 2740 QB, the two successful claimants sought basic and aggravated damages for false imprisonment and assault by police officers. Their claim for aggravated damages relied upon racial abuse and humiliation inflicted by the police officers. The basic awards for false imprisonment and assault were, for each claimant, £200 (false imprisonment, claimant 1) and £4,500 (false imprisonment, claimant 2). To these basic awards were added aggravated damages, calculated in accordance with the *Vento* principles for basic awards of discrimination, of £2,300 (claimant 1) and £7,200 (claimant 2).

II. HARASSMENT

1. HEADS OF DAMAGE

(1) *Non-pecuniary loss*

41–019   NOTE 81: Add at the end of the note: The award in *Saxton v Bayliss* Unreported 31 January 2014 Central London County Court, for harassment of an old lady by her very unpleasant neighbours causing her profound distress, the neighbours mounting a prolonged and vicious campaign to get her out of her house and thereby eliminate her right of way over their property, was £25,000. It would have been even higher in the absence of an additional exemplary award of £10,000.

DEFAMATION

II. SLANDERS ACTIONABLE *PER SE* AND LIBEL

1. LEVEL OF AWARDS

Insert a new paragraph after para.44–028:

The tide, however, of cautious judicial awards in trials without a jury remains **44–028A** strong, especially with the desire for consistency with awards for personal injury. In *Umeyor v Mwakamma* [2015] EWHC 2980 QB, a libellous publication was published to an unincorporated association of 50 to 60 members dedicated to the interests and welfare of the Mbaise community of which the claimant was a member. The allegation was of forgery but the claimant proved no financial loss and rumours had already abounded. The claimant was awarded only £2000 in general damages for injury to reputation and feelings despite the acknowledgement by Jay J at [92] that "attribution of forgery to the Claimant's is not something which may lightly be disregarded".

2. HEADS OF DAMAGE

(3) *The need for vindication*

Insert a new paragraph after para.44–033:

44–033A   The growth of the head of damages to vindicate reputation has, ironically, occurred at the same time as the decline, and ultimate rejection in *R (Lumba) v Secretary of State for the Home Department* [2012] 1 A.C. 245, of the concept of "vindicatory damages". The references to damages to "vindicate" in defamation cases are probably better understood as shorthand references for losses suffered for distress as well as the prospect of future consequences if the libel "emerges from its lurking place at some future date": *Broome v Cassell & Co Ltd* [1972] A.C. 1027, 1071 (Lord Hailsham). In an electronic age involving prolific means of dissemination of information the latter award can be of great importance. An approach which is becoming increasingly common is for an award to be made which instinctively synthesises existing distress as well as the prospect of future distress and future consequences (see *Cairns v Modi* [2012] EWCA Civ 1382; [2013] 1 W.L.R. 1015, 1027 [38]). For instance, in *Oyston v Reed* [2016] EWHC 1067, the defendant posted material concerning the chairman of Blackpool Football Club on a website which was read by many fans of the football club. His conduct aggravated the distress caused by the posting and the trial judge, Langstaff J, referred to all the factors including a reference to "vindication" and awarded a single sum of £30,000.

CHAPTER 45

INVASION OF PRIVACY

Add at the end of the paragraph: Now the Court of Appeal in *Google Inc v* **45–001**
Vidal-Hall [2015] EWCA Civ 311 has concluded that misuse of private information should be recognised as a tort (*ibid.* at [51]), being a civil wrong without any equitable characteristics (*ibid.* at [43]). It was so held there for the purposes of service out of the jurisdiction (*ibid.* at [51]) but should have general application. For the case in relation to breach of confidence and confidential information, see para.46–026, below.

1. Heads of Damage

(1) *Pecuniary loss*

Delete the words ", admittedly only by a majority of six to three" and replace **45–007**
with "by majority, subsequently reaffirmed in *R (O) v Secretary of State for the Home Department (Bail for Immigration Detainees)* [2016] UKSC 19; [2016] 1 W.L.R. 1717".

Add at the end of the paragraph: And as we saw in the chapter on vindicatory damages, they may also have been implicitly recognised in *Representative Claimants (Gulati) v MGN Ltd* [2015] EWCA Civ 1291 by an award of damages for the loss of a *right* to control information. However, in that case the Court of Appeal denied that the award was one to vindicate the right and some remarks by the Court suggest that it might best be understood as an award of restitutionary damages.

NOTE 46: Add at the end of the note: As pointed out in para.51–044, below, **45–008**
the primary purpose behind the introduction of a 10 per cent uplift in damages for non-pecuniary loss was to compensate those funding their claims by a conditional fee agreement for their inability, on success, to recover the success fee

from the defendant where the conditional fee agreement was entered into after the costs-amending legislation came into force on 1 April 2013. The judge's refusal of the uplift in the class action entitled *Gulati v MGN Ltd* [2015] EWHC 1482 Ch (facts at para.45–008A, below) was on account of success fees still being available to the several claimants (see *ibid.* at [165]). This can only be on the basis that the claimants' conditional fee agreements dated from before 1 April 2013. Yet that this was so does not appear anywhere in the overlong judgment delivered in late May 2015.

Insert a new paragraph after para.45–008:

45–008A The road to higher awards has led to dramatic increases in the class action entitled *Gulati v MGN Ltd* [2015] EWHC 1482 Ch. Eight claimants sued for invasion of their privacy which came about by the hacking of their phones by journalists who listened to their voicemails on a daily basis over several years and then reported on what they heard in very many articles addressed to the public. The awards made by Mann J started at £72,500 and moved through the £100,000s to a top award of more than £260,000. What also led to these awards being out of line with previous awards was that Mann J was giving compensation for loss of a right to control private information as well as for the more conventional injury to feelings. An appeal to the Court of Appeal on different points was dismissed: *Representative Claimants (Gulati) v MGN Ltd* [2015] EWCA Civ 1291 (on which see paras. 6–016 and 14–021, above).

CHAPTER 46

ECONOMIC TORTS

IV. BREACH, OR MISUSE, OF CONFIDENTIAL INFORMATION

NOTE 147: Substitute "below" with "above".   **46–026**

Add at the end of the paragraph: However, in *Google Inc v Vidal-Hall* [2015] EWCA Civ 311 the Court of Appeal was of the view, contrary to what is said in this paragraph in the main text, that *Kitechnology BV v Unicor GmbH Plast-maschinen* [1995] F.S.R. 765 CA, by which the Court of Appeal considered itself bound, established that an action for breach of confidence is not an action in tort. It can be argued that what was said to this effect was obiter as the Court of Appeal held that the case before it was not one of breach of confidence but one of misuse of private information, which it held to be indeed a tort: see the chapter dealing with invasion of privacy at para.45–001, above. The concepts of confidence and privacy were said not to be the same and protected different interests: *ibid.* at [21]; actions for breach of confidence and actions for misuse of private information were said to rest on different legal foundations: *ibid.* at [25].

Remove the final sentence prior to note 173. After note 173 insert the   **46–028** following: The strike out application had concerned the claimant's pleading for an enquiry as to damages following the findings of liability. At the subsequent enquiry, the primary judge allowed a claim for damages for lost profits from the directly infringing products only. The decision of the Court of Appeal is considered below because it is an example of where the first and the third types of damages were assessed in the same claim.

46–031   NOTE 184: Add at the end of the note: In *Primary Group (UK) Ltd v Royal Bank of Scotland Plc* [2014] EWHC 1082 Ch the same trial judge, Arnold J, approached the assessment of damages against a bank sued for breach of confidence by an insurance company in the same way as he had in the *Force India* case (see [181] et seq. of a long judgment), but the breach of confidence was a contractual one.

Insert a new paragraph after para.46–032:

46–032A   The decision of the Court of Appeal in *MVF 3 Aps & Ors v Bestnet Europe Ltd* [2016] EWCA Civ 541 is a case where all three types of damages claims were considered. The primary decision involved an enquiry as to damages arising from the defendants' production of mosquito nets that used the confidential information as well as damages for the defendants' production of nets that did not involve misuse of confidential information but were indirectly derived from the use of the confidential information. In relation to the nets which were derived from the misuse of confidential information the primary judge allowed (i) damages for lost profits on sales that the claimant would have made as well as (ii) damages on the "user principle" for sales that the claimant could not prove that it would have made with a royalty rate of 4 per cent. The Court of Appeal upheld these conclusions. As to the latter, the rate for the use of the confidential information was restitutionary because it focused on the price that the defendants had to pay. The Court of Appeal emphasised that considerations unique to the claimant were irrelevant. However, the primary judge declined to award damages for lost profits for the nets which were indirectly derived from the misuse of confidential information. Instead, for those nets the primary judge awarded a "quasi-consultancy" fee to reflect the extent to which the sales of those nets were brought about by the use of confidential information. The Court of Appeal also upheld this conclusion. As to the lost profits from the indirectly derived nets, Floyd LJ, with whom Lindblom LJ and Sir Colin Rimer agreed, explained that the law would not impose liability for all the consequences of the wrongful action ([90]). Essentially, those profits were beyond the scope of liability for consequences because the sales were not wrongful. The proper measure of damages for the indirectly derived nets was the consultancy fee because this reflected "the sort of assistance" which the defendants needed when, having breached the duty of confidence, they sought to use that information to develop the later nets. Again the award is restitutionary because it focuses upon the price that the defendants would have had to pay for the type of assistance that they received.

V. INFRINGEMENT OF RIGHTS IN INTELLECTUAL PROPERTY

2. The Present English Law, the Directive Apart

(3) *Infringement of copyright and design right*

Insert a new note before the "and" ending the third line of the paragraph: **46–054**

NOTE 326a: Damages have also been measured by a licence fee where the number of lost sales has been too speculative and too open to inaccuracy to be a sound basis for calculation. This was done in *Kohler Mira Ltd v Bristan Group Ltd* [2014] EWHC 1931 (IPEC), which concerned infringement of design right in electric shower units.

Add at the end of the paragraph: Yet it was held in *Kohler Mira Ltd v Bristan* **46–057**
Group Ltd [2014] EWHC 1931 (IPEC) that the claimant who had established infringement of design right in electric shower units was in principle entitled to damages in relation to products unprotected by the design right infringed if the damage was caused by the infringement, was foreseeable, and was not excluded by public policy: see *ibid.* at [28] et seq.

Add at the end of the paragraph: In *Pendle Metalwares Ltd v Walter Page* **46–064**
(Safeway's) Ltd [2014] EWHC 1140 Ch, His Honour Judge Purle awarded additional damages on account of the flagrancy of the infringement but refused them in respect of benefit accruing by reason of the infringement: see *ibid.* at [46]–[52].

3. The Impact of the European Directive

(1) *Range of application*

NOTE 399: Add at the end of the note: In *Kohler Mira Ltd v Bristan Group* **46–071**
Ltd [2014] EWHC 1931 (IPEC), which concerned infringement of design right in electric shower units, it was appreciated that moral prejudice referred to non-pecuniary loss. The 10 per cent uplift asked for on the award given for pecuniary loss was therefore refused as there was no non-pecuniary loss. Non-pecuniary loss, it was rightly said, was likely to arise only in very particular circumstances: *ibid.* at [60]

MISREPRESENTATION

I. FRAUDULENT MISREPRESENTATION: DECEIT

2. Heads of Damage

(1) *Pecuniary loss*

Insert a new paragraph after para.47–019:

On the other hand, this does not mean that subsequent events will always be **47–019A** relevant for the purpose of quantifying damages. In *OMV Petrom SA v Glencore International AG* [2016] EWCA Civ 778, the party which committed the fraud attempted to rely on subsequent events to show that the real value of the product was not substantially eroded by the fraudulent misrepresentations. Glencore supplied oil to Petrom which resembled the type of oil which it had promised to supply but which was actually a cheaper substitute. Glencore created a suite of false documents to conceal its deceit. Petrom claimed as damages the price that it had paid of around US $434 million less the value of the oil at the date it was supplied. The trial judge awarded around US $40 million. The value of the oil was discounted to reflect the fact that a purchaser would not pay the value of an untried blend which could affect the machinery, or cause rust or fire. Glencore submitted that since nothing untoward occurred, any discount is inappropriate because to allow a discount would be to compensate Petrom for a loss which it might have suffered but did not ([31]). In the Court of Appeal, Christopher Clarke LJ (with whom Kitchin and Black LJJ agreed) rejected this submission on the basis that the failure of the risk to materialise after the date of acquisition of the oil was to be disregarded. One reason for this was that otherwise Glencore could recover a price which it would not have recovered if it had been honest. In any event, evidence of a lack of deleterious consequences was a matter for Glencore to prove if it asserted that none had arisen: *The World Beauty* [1970] P. 144, 154; *Midco v Piper* [2004] EWCA Civ 476.

BOOK SIX

PROCEDURE

APPEALS

■

II. APPEALS FROM AN AWARD OF DAMAGES BY A JUDGE

2. GROUNDS FOR REASSESSING THE DAMAGES

(2) *Entirely erroneous estimate*

Add at the end of the paragraph: In all instances, this 10 per cent uplift is not **51–044**
discretionary—Courts must award it in all cases except conditional fee arrange-
ments, even if it gives a claimant a windfall: *Summers v Bundy* [2016] EWCA
Civ 126.